Ingo Bernhardt

A CASE FOR CHANGE

FMCG: Winning the
commercial battle
in emerging markets

A Case For Change

First edition 2015,
spraybooks facts 01
Copyright © of this edition
spraybooks publishing, 2015,
Cologne, Germany
Copyright © Ingo Bernhardt, 2015

Editing: Tobias Nickel

Printed by CreateSpace

For further information address
spraybooks publishing,
Verlag Bielfeldt + Bürger GbR
Remigiusstr. 20, 50999 Koeln, Germany.

info@spraybooks.com
www.spraybooks.com

ISBN 978-3-945684-99-3

Ingo Bernhardt

A Case For Change

INHALT

This work would not have been possible without the career opportunities that I was offered and, even more so, the great support from my family. Many vacations and weekends later now, I would like to dedicate this book to my wife Birgit and my daughters Sarah and Nina.

PREFACE

»Someone's sitting in the shade today because someone planted a tree a long time ago.«

— Warren Buffett

CASE FOR CHANGE is a textbook from practitioners for practitioners. The author has a commercial track record of working with global *Fast Moving Consumer Goods* (FMCG) companies in more than forty countries, most of them developing or emerging countries.

Designed to meet the needs of business school students, as well as of those who already work in the consumer goods industry, this book provides insights into the operational procedures of several globally operating *consumer packaged goods companies* (CPG) that have managed to succeed in these markets over and over again. Complementing brand marketing, a scientific approach to commercial planning and commercial execution continues to be today's driving force behind sustainable profitability, even in markets with low purchasing power.

This book forms the foundation of the CASE FOR CHANGE program. This program is designed to complement the content of this book with additional examples and how-tos through Business school lectures and a series of webinars for self-training.

QR 1

In 2020, emerging and developing markets will represent about 70% (QR 1) of FMCG' sales and profits (see fig. 1).

QR 2

Future FMCG growth will primarily be driven by the growth of urban populations in emerging countries. In 2020, about 60% of the top 600 cities will be located in emerging countries (QR 2) and 735 million households, or 1.3 billion consumers (QR 3), will belong to the new middle class that can afford to consume global brands.

QR 3

For FMCG companies of various sizes, revenue and profit distribution has already started to shift in favor of developing and emerging markets.

This book sets out to provide the specific commercial skills required to succeed in these markets based on the author's many years of experience in senior commercial roles at global FMCG companies.

Whereas global players have sufficient resources to capture and disseminate commercial learnings into new markets, smaller players often have different structures and less formal capacity building opportunities to be applied to markets of the future.

This book is designed to help small and medium sized FMCG companies with international brands to succeed commercially in these important future markets.

One may be inclined to think that making branded products available as fast as possible by using local distribution partners or wholesalers may be the way to success, but this is short-term thinking.

While speed to market and ubiquity are important, experience has shown that building a basic understanding of the right commercial planning and execution within the own local organization and among commercial partners on site will help companies to grow profitably – once the first battles are won!

Studying companies that have a history of commercial success in these markets, as well as a long learning curve, will allow smaller companies to succeed.

This book proposes a commercial framework of operational and strategic planning and execution that builds on publicly available business cases of the past ten to fifteen years. These cases illustrate the commercial success that global FMCG companies, such as Procter & Gamble, Unilever, Coca-Cola or Nestlé, have had in developing and emerging markets.

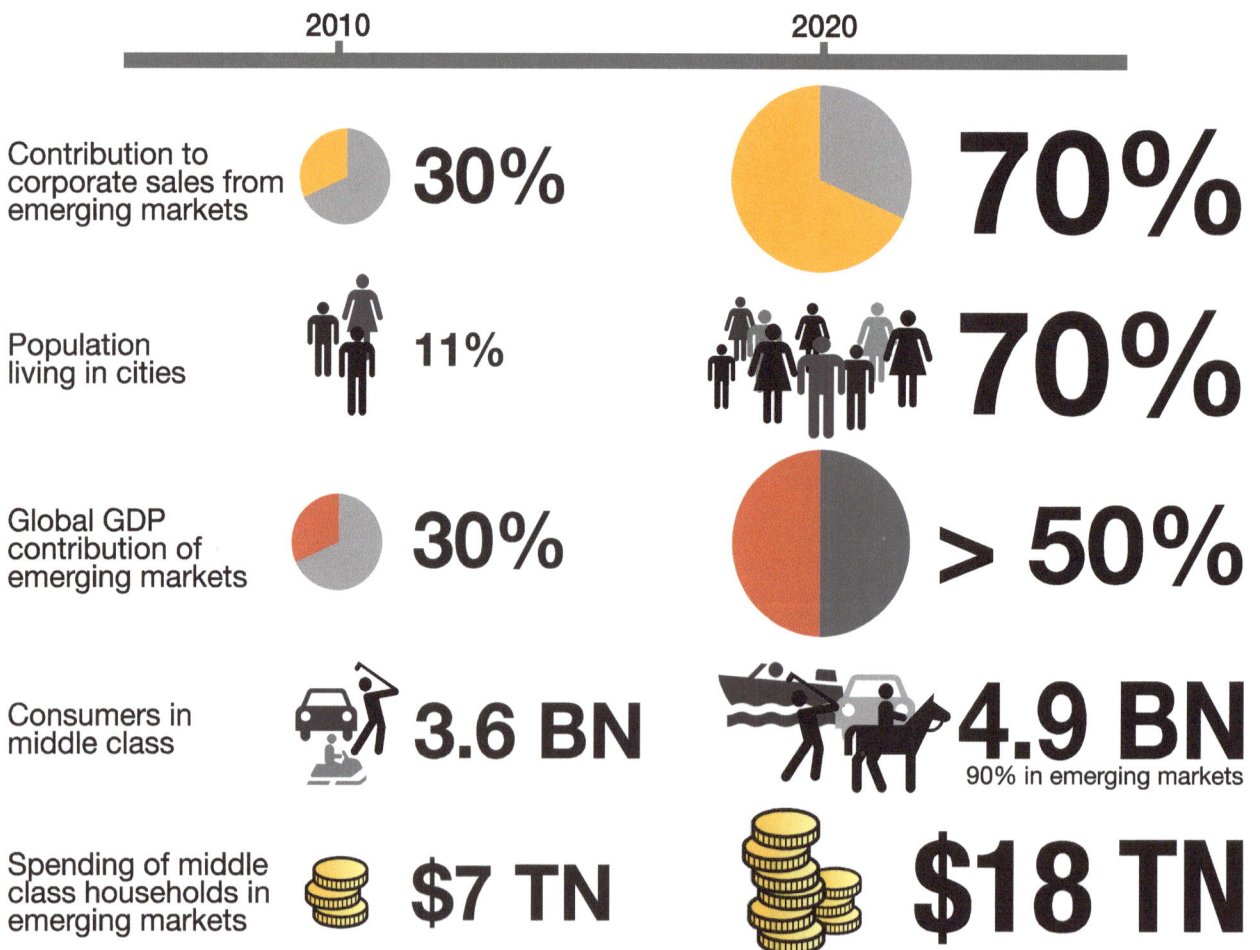

	2010	2020
Contribution to corporate sales from emerging markets	30%	70%
Population living in cities	11%	70%
Global GDP contribution of emerging markets	30%	> 50%
Consumers in middle class	3.6 BN	4.9 BN — 90% in emerging markets
Spending of middle class households in emerging markets	$7 TN	$18 TN

Fig. 1 — Over time

TECHNOLOGY, LANGUAGE AND MOBILITY

Technology, language and increased mobility globalize all businesses. Simple, electronic communication available 24/7 and in one single language, English, has become the norm. In addition, global IT solutions, such as SAP and Oracle, have become implemented across the world.

Global infrastructure and improved local education levels, combined with the ease of communication, have enabled globally operating companies to learn and disseminate learning swiftly across their different geographical locations. Against the backdrop of these developments over the past ten years, even the most local commercial exchanges have started to become as globalized as other business functions before.

However, even for global brands, it is still true that all business is local and that consumer needs continue to vary significantly from one geographical location to another.

In spite of this, most successful global Consumer Packaged Goods (CPG) companies have built a commercial muscle that can be applied immediately to all new markets to improve commercial performance locally.

Furthermore, improved high bandwidth communication technology, lower cost of travel and improved global language capabilities have led to a dramatic increase in global mobility of associates within large consumer goods manufacturers.

The learning curve, experienced when moving into a new market, is significantly less steep today. Therefore, the exchange of talent has become easier and more frequent, even on the lower middle management level. Developing and emerging countries have greatly benefited from importing and exporting talent.

The ability to connect anytime and from anywhere, as well as higher talent mobility, has helped developing and emerging markets to catch up and even surpass commercial capabilities of developed markets, such as the U.S. or Europe.

This book is specifically designed to help FMCG companies of a smaller scale that have a smaller library of corporate learning or less resources dedicated to building and distributing commercial skills. The goal is to expand their commercial planning and execution capabilities.

This book focuses on developing and emerging markets. For lack of a widely recognized definition, the terms developing or emerging markets are used when referring to a group of markets outside of affluent developed markets. For the past fifty years, developed countries have dominated the global economy. In spite of accounting for only twenty percent of the world's population, developed countries have contributed about 70-80% of global income. A situation that will likely change over the next twenty years, as will be discussed in the next section.

SEVENTY PERCENT OF GROWTH

Among business leaders, as well as politicians there is a common understanding that FMCG companies' main source of growth over the next twenty years (QR 4) will come from developing or emerging markets.

Bain Consultancy states that by 2015 (QR 5) markets like China, India, Brazil, Turkey will contribute approximately 60% of global GDP and 60% of retail growth. In contrast, today five markets make up 30% of global GDP (U.S., UK, Canada, France, Germany).

Citing from a recent McKinsey report (QR 6):

»Over the past ten years fifty key categories of FMCG grew by 5% annually to reach seven trillion Dollars. Spending in emerging markets will drive the expected increase in consumer spending worldwide. By 2020, emerging markets will represent close to 50% of total consumer spending and about 70% of the overall growth in consumer spending from 2010 to 2020.«

QR 4

QR 5

QR 6

URBAN AREAS: THE NUMBER ONE DRIVER OF GROWTH

Today, only six hundred urban centers worldwide generate about 60% of global GDP. Their contribution will remain unchanged, but the composition and location of these cities will shift towards the South and – even more decisively – the East. By 2020, roughly 70% of the world's population (QR 7) will live in urban areas.

MIDDLE CLASS HOUSEHOLD

There is no uniform way of defining a middle class household (QR 8). According to one narrow definition, the middle class includes all households with an annual income above $31,000 PPP (Purchase Power Parity adjusted, QR 9) or a daily income of about $85.

Milanovic and Yitzhaki developed a more popular definition, which holds that the *global middle class* starts at an annual income of only $4,000 (in $ PPP of 2005).

Conservatively estimated there were 3.6 billion middle class consumers in developing countries in 2010. This number is expected to grow by an additional 1.3 billion consumers by 2020, that is, 250,000 to 300,000 new middle class households per day. (See fig. 1).

More recent studies (QR 10) that base their estimates on cars in circulation even indicate that the number of current middle class households is 50-60% larger.

Although middle class consumers in developing and emerging countries are still considerably poorer than their counterparts in advanced economies, their vast number and increasing ability to devote more of their income to consumer goods will grow the market enormously. It has been estimated that middle class households will spend an additional 10 trillion dollars by 2020 (QR 11).

SOURCE OF PROFIT

Today, global FMCG, such as Unilever, Coca-Cola, Gillette, Nestlé and Colgate-Palmolive, generate one third or more of their revenue from these markets, with profitability being equal to, or higher than, what they achieve in developed economies.

For example, the Coca-Cola Company now derives 37% of its revenue (QR 12) from Latin America, Africa and Asia, and these markets contribute a stunning 49% to Coca-Cola's operating profits. Similarly, the Colgate-Palmolive Company receives 45% of its revenue and nearly half of its operating income from these markets.

Large consumer goods companies, such as Procter & Gamble or Unilever, estimate that, by 2020, 70% of their sales will come from developing markets. Today, these markets account for 50% of their sales.

In 2011, Heinz' CEO Bill Johnson said that 20% of revenues come from emerging markets, whereas in previous years it had only been 5%.

At the same time, emerging countries are likely to skip development stages that other markets had to go through, thus accelerating their progress even more. With relatively basic infrastructure and yet high quality affordable Internet coverage, these markets derive a disproportionately high advantage from modern technology.

A good example of this trend (QR 13) is South Korea (2012 GDP PPP $32,000, 1960 PPP $11,000). which forty years ago was among the poorest countries of the world.

Today, South Korea ranks number twelve in GDP per capita and dominates the global smart phone market, establishing itself as the global leader in smart phone penetration, broadband availability and mobile downloads.

QR 13

CASE FOR CHANGE

»In a world where populations are growing, where natural resources are stressed, where communities are forced to do more with less and where consumers' expectations are expanding, sustainability is core to our business continuity and survival.«

— Muhtar Kent,
The Coca-Cola Company, 2010,
QR 14

QR 14

SUPPORT BROADER TARGETS

This book describes world-class commercial work. However, commercial work is only one of multiple functions in most FMCG companies. Commercial planning, as the author would like it to be seen, works side-by-side with other critical functions, such as marketing, finance, human resources, manufacturing and sales.

This book furthermore assumes that any fast-moving consumer good company, typically needs to satisfy a variety of stakeholders:

- Shareholders;
- Employees;
- Communities and environment, in which the company operates;
- Customers of this company.

This book demonstrates how the commercial function supports the growth of traditional targets of any company, such as revenue, share and ROIC. This helps fulfill shareholder expectations.

All large companies and organizations, irrelevant of their industry and irrelevant of their profit or non-profit status, have to assume responsibilities that go beyond traditional targets.

- Sustainability: A company only acts responsibly and sustainably if business is conducted in an environmentally friendly way. A great example of a sustainable company is the Coca-Cola Corporation. Together with the World Wide Fund for Nature (WWF), this company has implemented a water neutral principle (QR 15), pledging to return as much water to the world as it uses;
- People: Everything an organization does has to improve the living conditions of its employees, customers and consumers, as well as benefit the communities in which business is conducted;
- Community: The responsibility of benefiting these communities includes: enhancing the well-being of the people, improving access to natural resources and stimulating economic growth. Good examples of such community development

QR 16

projects are Coca-Cola's Ekocenters (QR 16) or mini one-stop shops that will supply cooked meals, clean water, power, Internet, vaccines and beverages to twenty developing countries.

In many multinational companies, the commercial function contributes to these targets just as much as to traditional economic targets.

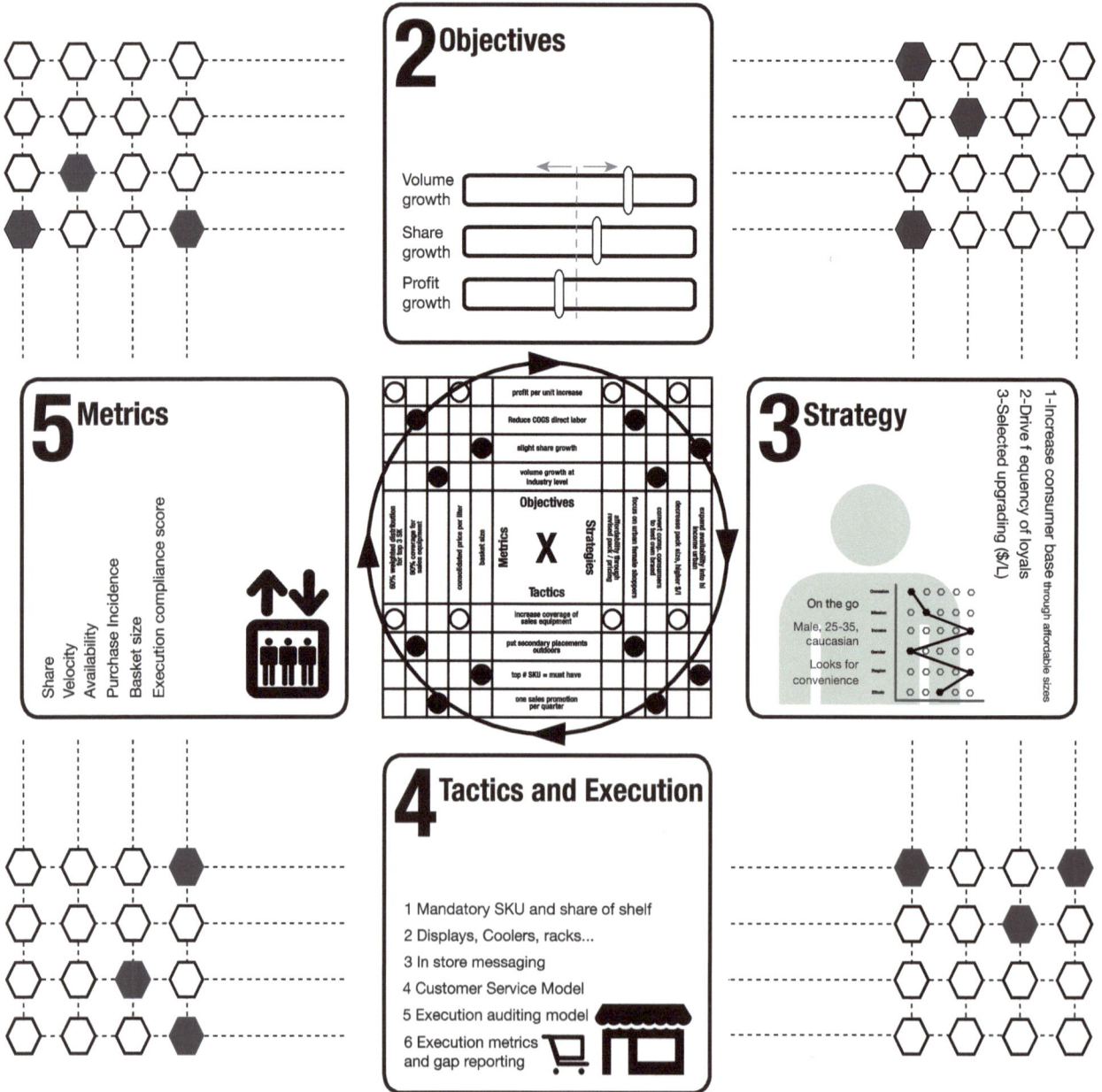

2 Objectives

Volume growth
Share growth
Profit growth

5 Metrics

Share
Velocity
Availability
Purchase Incidence
Basket size
Execution compliance score

3 Strategy

1-Increase consumer base through affordable sizes
2-Drive f equency of loyals
3-Selected upgrading ($/L)

On the go
Male, 25-35, caucasian
Looks for convenience

4 Tactics and Execution

1 Mandatory SKU and share of shelf
2 Displays, Coolers, racks...
3 In store messaging
4 Customer Service Model
5 Execution auditing model
6 Execution metrics and gap reporting

Objectives
Metrics X Strategies
Tactics

profit per unit increase
Reduce COGS direct labor
slight share growth
volume growth at industry level

increase coverage of sales equipment
put secondary placements outdoors
top # SKU = must have
one sales promotion per quarter

Fig. 2 — The Closed Commercial Loop™

INTRODUCTION

A CASE FOR CHANGE is divided into six chapters. In sequence, this book describes five interconnected commercial disciplines, which together are called the Closed Commercial Loop™ (see fig. 2). Before describing each of the chapters and the suggested workflow, the scope of planning will be defined.

PLANNING SCOPE

Two dimensions define the scope of commercial planning:

- Short-term versus long-term — is it a one-year operational plan or a three-year strategic plan?
- Granularity of planning.

SHORT-TERM AND LONGER-TERM

Longer-term planning, which this book defines as three-year strategic planning, takes place primarily on the top level, i.e. the national level. Short-term and long-term plans — both include specific disciplines. Compare Table 1, which maps out elements of short- and long-term planning in relation to each of the chapters of this book.

WORKING LEVEL

Chapter One determines the number of market segments for which planning and execution work is done. Segmentation, therefore, determines the working level and the amount of planning work.

- Default working level for the purpose of this book, refers to channel by category and is based on the author's commercial experience in over thirty countries (i.e. breakfast cereals in small traditional grocery stores)
- Top level refers to the national level
- Bottom level is SKU by (sub) channel.

STRUCTURE OF THE BOOK

Before diving into the different chapters, a short word on the book's style and structure and granularity. This book covers the totality of commercial planning and execution for students of business schools, as well as current CPG-practitioners, planning to increase their capabilities. It is meant to be taught in class or through self-teaching in a relatively short time. Complementing classic business economics literature, this book goes into more detail in those areas that are more practical in nature and less often found in academic literature. On the flip side, topics, which are already well covered in textbooks on marketing or sales, will only be referred to briefly. It is important to note that it remains critical to familiarize oneself with these disciplines. For example, the chapter on strategy mentions price elasticity for the purpose of determining promotional price points, but does not explain this concept in depth.

Other topics, such as segmentation or channel planning, are covered in more depth, providing tools that can be used immediately in the real world.

All chapters combined and in sequence form a closed and interconnected loop of commercial planning, execution, tracking and improvement. This the author refers to as the Closed Commercial Loop™ (see fig. 2).

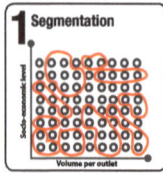

CHAPTER ONE

... deals with segmentation. Market segmentation determines the granularity of planning and has a direct impact on both marketing and commercial planning.

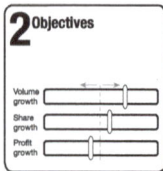

CHAPTER TWO

... is about setting objectives and categorizing them sequentially from the highest level to the lowest level. Chapter Two marks the starting point of the Closed Commercial Loop™.

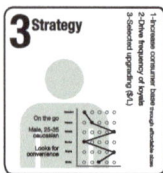

CHAPTER THREE

... describes how to use strategies in order to bring the objectives developed in the previous chapter to life. It also shows how to create a bundle of tactics in each segment to support the segment objectives. The second part of Chapter Three focuses on assortment and pricing. Outside of tactical, promotional pricing the combination of brand, packaging and pricing is a strategic decision, because of its long-term implications and lead times.

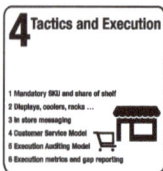

CHAPTER FOUR

... explains how to identify commercial tactics, which are effective in supporting all the previous chapters on profile strategies and objectives. The mix of assortment, promotional activities and in-store messaging is captured in an activation blue print.

CHAPTER FIVE

... is the final chapter of the Closed Commercial Loop™. It covers the setting of metrics required to measure the performance of previously described tactics and their execution. These metrics are ultimately linked back to objective setting and tactic revision.

CHAPTER SIX

... introduces a supportive spreadsheet tool, which summarizes all previous steps, their sub elements, and connectors in a turnkey Microsoft Excel tool.

LINE OF SIGHT

This book takes a look across existing successful practices and combines selected learnings and ideas into one logical framework. This framework (see fig. 2) provides a line of sight from every single tactical and executive metric back to the company's strategy.

For confidential reasons, this book does not represent a single business case or mirror a specific best practice. Instead, it applies the author's 25-year experience with global FMCG companies in developing and emerging markets and merges this with available publications.

THE TASTE COMPANY OF »EMERGIA«

The fictitious country of »Emergia« (somewhere in Central Asia) and a local subsidiary of »The Taste Company« (TTC), a global player in ice cream, serve as examples throughout most chapters in this book.

All data relative to TTC is purely illustrative, while, at the same time, the TTC case serves as a good representation of commercial situations that consumer goods companies would likely face in emerging markets. The TTC case demonstrates how processes, data and tools should be utilized to create meaningful and tangible outputs for each of the chapters in this book.

TTC examples and exercises all utilize information summarized on a one-page fact sheet, which the reader is suggested to download (Download fact sheet as PDF, QR 17, or Excel file, QR 18).

QR 17 PDF

QR 18 Excel

Emergia is a central Asian market with single digit GDP growth rates and stagnating net-income growth. During the first couple of years, availability increases stimulated consumption, but now per capita consumption is not growing as strong anymore.

»The Taste Company« focuses on various categories within consumer ice cream and other related product categories. TTC's competitive advantage, both in brand strength and production technology, lies within a unique form of soft ice.

The current per capita consumption of TTC branded ice cream is five portions, meaning five consumptions annually of a 50g personalized ice cream portion.

TTC, Emergia reports to TTC's regional headquarters for Central Asia, where brand marketing and many other business functions are concentrated for the various markets in the region. However, there is no regional commercial function and, as a result, TTC Emergia has the license and obligation to act independently.

After having been four years in the market, TTC is now planning for its fifth year in Emergia.

When TTC entered the market, they became market leaders within six months. Since then many local manufacturers with much lower cost structures have used fast copy/paste launches to enter the market. Now, TTC's revenue share is tied with their number one competitor, »EM foods«.

TTC's top brand "Daily" has brand preference scores 20% up in comparison to »EM foods« brands. Daily average consumer pricing is at a 25% premium against »EM foods«.

TTC has a tradition and an expectation to defend market leadership and to build a sustainable, profitable business in Emergia.

During the first four years, TTC over-invested in its key brand and in commercialization. For the upcoming planning period, the profit and loss parameters that have been agreed upon with the regional headquarter are as follows:

- Gross profit: 50% of net sales;
- Marketing / Commercial budgets: 8% of net sales;
- Operating profit target: 10%.

Based on the TTC case, this book will establish the foundation of a one-year operational commercial plan, leveraging the data provided in the fact sheet and applying the tools from the textbook.

WORKFLOW

The suggested workflow is identical for all commercial work. What to include, however, depends largely on whether the assignment is an operational (one-year) plan or a strategic (three-plus years) plan. Refer to Table 1 for an overview of the workflow for short-term and long-term planning.

Workflow starts once the segmentation work (Chapter One) has defined the level of planning/execution granularity.

WORKFLOW: ONE-YEAR PLAN

- Fine-tune segmentation;
- Set low-level KBI;
- Fine-tune activation blueprint;
- Fine-tune execution tracking;
- Adapt customer service model;
- Develop tactics;
- Create metrics for tactics and link back to "objectives".

Chapter	Subchapter	1-year plan	3-year plan
Segmentation		fine tune for specific communication or promotinal activities	create new / review in depth
	long term	included from 3-yr plan	high level KBI on national or channel level
Objectives	operational	low level KBI	not included
	identify strategic growth opportunities	not included	review regularly
	profiles and roles	not included	review regularly
	growth strategies	not included	review regularly
Strategies	activation blueprint	fine-tune annually	create new / review in depth
	execution tracking	fine-tune annually	create new / review in depth
	customer service model	fine-tune annually	create new / review in depth

Table 1 — Short and long term planning elements

WORKFLOW: THREE-YEAR PLAN

- In-depth review of segmentation;
- Setting/adapting high-level KBI for national and channel level;
- Determine Strategic Growth Opportunities (SGO);
- Review channel roles and channel profiles;
- Develop strategies to leverage SGO;
- Build/review activation blueprint;
- Review execution tracking model;
- Review customer service model.

RUNNING THE CLOSED COMMERCIAL LOOP™ FOR THE FIRST TIME

Start the long-term process in a small group of two, at most three, associates with experience in marketing, general management or commercial work.

Start at the high-level and use the teams' combined business judgment to fill potential data gaps. By nature, this work will serve a rather directional purpose and is neither perfect nor will it replace the use of detailed, concrete data.

NOTE

For the purpose of simplicity and to illustrate the methodology, the described process in this book assumes a simple segmentation of (trade) channels – similar to the segmentation described in our example of TTC in Emergia. Consequently, the next chapters in the Closed Commercial Loop™ will refer to channel objectives, channel strategies and channel tactics.

Also, for simplicity reasons, this book assumes only one product category. Most global consumer manufacturers, of course, have multiple product categories and brands within categories.

When using the commercial loop for the first time, this approach will help to become more familiar with the process and will help to precisely determine the scope and granularity of the data requirements. During this process, make sure not to get stuck in details, such as assortment or pricing details.

Once the small team has gone through the Closed Commercial Loop™ at the high level, it kicks off the process with detailed data. It is also necessary to set up project teams responsible for each channel for the entire process.

Consequently, work through all chapters for 1-2 segments in parallel. This approach ensures efficiency and helps to compare the different channels during the exercises.

In a real life situation, the number of plans equals the number of channels multiplied by the number of categories, i.e. three channels times two categories equals six plans (see fig. 3).

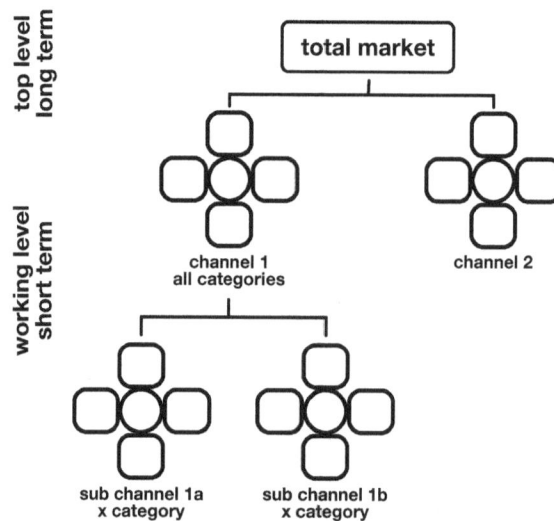

top level
long term

working level
short term

total market

channel 1
all categories

channel 2

sub channel 1a
x category

sub channel 1b
x category

Fig. 3 — Planning granularity - 3 plan example

SEGMENTATION

»Cause division among them. Attack when they are unprepared, make your move when they do not expect it.«

— Sun Tzu

SEGMENTATION: A STRATEGIC WEAPON

Segmenting, or dividing the market, reduces a common risk of manufacturers of mass or commodity categories, namely:

- The gradual decline of profit margins as competition increases and
- Copycats take share.

This chapter consists of the following parts:

- Segmentation as the base for differentiation;
- Degree of segmentation;
- Potential conflict between segmentation and horizontal or vertical growth strategies;
- Potential downsides of segmentation;
- The how-to of segmentation;
- Requirements for good segmentation;
- Data sources.

As Michael E. Porter states in What is Strategy? (QR 19):

»A company can outperform rivals only if it can establish a difference that it can preserve. It must deliver greater value to customers or create comparable value at lower cost, or both. [...] Delivering greater value allows a company to charge higher average unit prices.«

Differentiation, when well planned and executed from a marketing and commercial side, leads to:

- Higher average prices per unit (see fig. 4: Volume and profit);
- Decreased vulnerability to economic downturns;
- Long-term competitive advantages.

Segmentation is the base and the key enabler of differentiation. It is a continuum from zero (no differentiation, same offer everywhere) to

QR 19

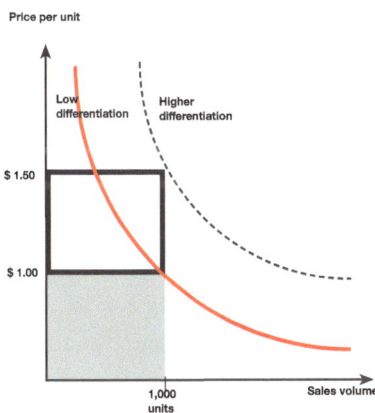

Fig. 4 — Volume and profit

infinite (every consumer gets a tailor made product, i.e. in tailoring). Also see fig. 5, which displays a typical evolution of market segmentation.

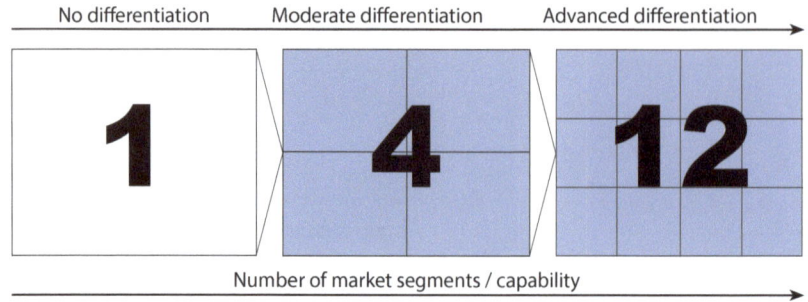

Fig. 5 — Continuum of segments

More practically: the total market is broken down into segments or clusters, each addressing needs that are sufficiently different from each other. See fig. 6.

Differentiation in this book is used to describe the practice of offering IDENTICAL product quality (i.e. fresh milk) at DIFFERENT price points and/or in different packaging and different shopper messaging to meet the needs of different shoppers and consumers in distinct segments.

Successful FMCG manufacturers are typically thriving of offering Differentiated Mass Products. Even in emerging markets, however, volume growth rates decline over time, as more and more competitors enter the market. Successful companies take the following steps to prevent this phenomenon: they build capabilities in times of steep volume growth, so that they can later increase their degree of pack/price differentiation, which in turn allows them to charge higher prices per unit, and thus creates incremental profit.

In addition to Michael E. Porter's teaching, all experience shows that differentiation leads to a strategic competitive edge and a culture that CPG manufacturers need to implement at an early stage in emerging markets. Only if the organization and its business partners have gradually built capabilities over years, then differentiation is an available strategic weapon once volume growth slows down or higher-income clusters appear in emerging markets.

As part of its three-year strategic plan, every FMCG company should review its balance of increased complexity, capabilities and level of differentiation. Most successful companies have gone through a seven- or eight-year journey of developing a sophisticated segmentation, starting with three segments initially and ending up with 60+ segments.

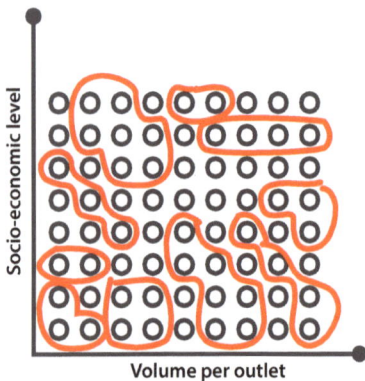

Fig. 6 — Segmentation principle

DEGREE OF SEGMENTATION

The degree of segmentation (see fig. 7) depends on:

- Product category: some products (i.e. like flower, fuel, sugar, paper towels) do not lend themselves to a strong degree of differentiation;
- Consumer price elasticity: the more generic a category, the more elastic consumer demand. Differentiation becomes more challenging with high elasticity;
- Capability to develop differentiated packaging (works less well with products such as energy);
- Number of different consumption situations, where the same product quality is being used (i.e. coffee has many different consumption occasions, detergent has only one);
- Ability to plan and execute differentiated offerings. Typically, the higher the degree of DSD (Direct store delivery), merchandising and in store activation, the higher the capabilities for segmented execution. The ability to adopt the Customer Service Model and to manage service costs is an approach (sales, distribution, activation) to market needs and to manage GoToMarket costs is a critical enabler for segmented execution.

POTENTIAL CONFLICTS AND DOWNSIDES

In Chapter Three, strategies will be divided into horizontal and vertical strategies (see fig. 24).

Horizontal strategies expand distribution into additional channels or outlets, whereas vertical strategies summarize all measures to grow same store sales in existing distribution. As segmentation is a key enabler for any vertical growth strategy, the relationship and potential trade-off between horizontal growth and segmentation should be explained.

Whereas vertical growth strategies build on segmentation (hence, very targeted activation), horizontal growth strategies require a one-size-fits-all offer to maintain the ability to expand and grow rapidly.

The benefits of segmentation are clear, but segmentation does come at a price:

- Overall increased business complexity;
- Higher number of pack or price variations;
- In-store activation or messaging variety grows with the complexity of pack/price variations;
- More time required with customers, more specialized customer service models may be required;
- More challenges in product delivery;
- Smaller production runs / reduced line utilization.

REQUIREMENTS FOR GOOD SEGMENTATION WORK

The objective of any segmentation work is to determine a number of segments that are sufficiently different in the sense that this difference is:

- Actionable (in store, customer service models);
- Sustainable (difficult to copy in a short time, financially scalable);
- Consumer and shopper relevant;
- Incremental profit exceeds incremental execution and other complexity costs.

Segmentation work, as it will be described later in this chapter, typically generates a very high number of segments at first. These then need to be consolidated to meet the capabilities of execution.

POTENTIAL SEGMENTATION CRITERIA TO CONSIDER

The previous section showed what "smart" segmentation looks like. Any segmentation requires equally smart criteria or perspectives by means of which to divide the market. A list of typical segmentation criteria are (see also fig. 8):

- Geographies, cultural differences, taste preferences;
- Retail channels;
- Retail size or store revenues;
- Socio-demographic data, incl. ethnics;
- Consumption occasion – why is a product purchased;
- Shopping Missions;
- Logistic infrastructure (i.e. availability of warehouses, roads, trucks in urban areas)

The most granular commercial segment would be a micro segment (i.e. one street, one house).

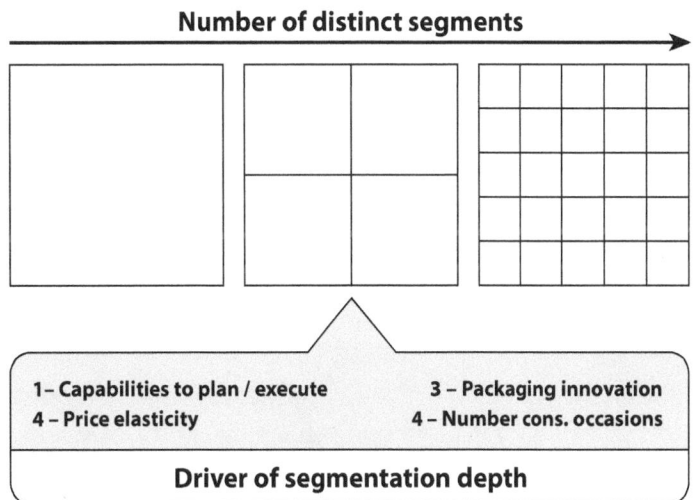

Number of distinct segments →

| 1– Capabilities to plan / execute | 3 – Packaging innovation |
| 4 – Price elasticity | 4 – Number cons. occasions |

Driver of segmentation depth

Fig. 7 — Degree and depth of segmentation

SEGMENTATION: A SIMPLE HOW-TO

Segmentation begins with in-depth data mining and cluster analysis. This includes all possibly accessible data points, insights or trends relative to the criteria listed in the previous section. A company should leverage all their primary or secondary research for this critical exercise and consider purchasing data where required.

As laid out in the workflow at the beginning of this book, segmentation needs to be reviewed for long-term planning and fine-tuned for the (one-year) operational plan. Some criteria evolve faster than others, while some data becomes available later. These criteria should be monitored regularly. Fig. 8 illustrates a simple three-step workflow.

Segmentation should start with a white sheet of paper and no segmentation in mind. Cluster analysis (QR 20) is the preferred statistical method for segmentation. Since this statistical methodology is well covered in other literature, this book will not explain it in more depth.

QR 20

Data Warehouse
geographies / delivery routes
ethnics / socio-demographics
sub categories / pack sizes
pricing elasticity
store formats
consumption / shopping patterns

Identify maximum number of segments to be executed based on imminent capabilities

Run cluster analysis to arrive at clusters that require different portfolio or pricing or activation matching the execution capabilities

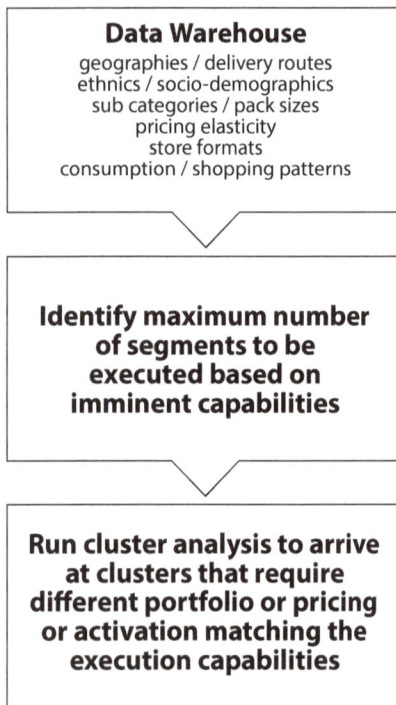

Fig. 8 — Segmentation workflow

SUGGESTED SEGMENTATION FOR EMERGING MARKETS

Assuming that differentiation capabilities and Direct Store Delivery (DSD) levels are still basic, segmentation needs to stay simple in the beginning and respect local data availability, as well as planning and execution capabilities.

Three criteria that are often used in emerging markets (start with number one, then combine number one and number two and later use all three) include (see fig. 11):

1. Basic channels (i.e. traditional grocery, organized retail, local on premise);
2. Store size, applying current and potential sales per store (SPS);
3. Socio-economic, using purchasing power.

Channel segmentation requires the channel planner to use the channel definition identical to what the local syndicated research (i.e. Nielsen) uses or to define segments himself (i.e. by store size, location, number of check outs...).

Store size segmentation: it is recommended to use a mix of current and potential Sales-per-Store (SPS) and to have three to five SPS clus-

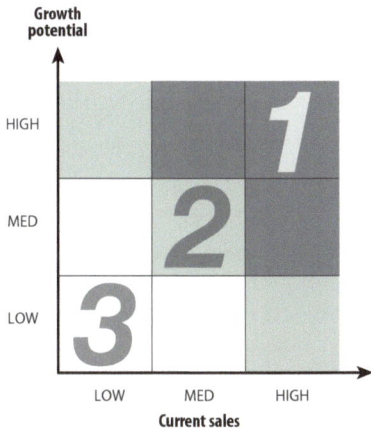

Fig. 9 — Current sales vs. potential

ters. Highest SPS represents typically 5-10% of customer base, yet 20-30% of total sales (see fig. 9 and fig. 10).

Socio-economic segmentation: once a market has successfully experienced channel and SPS segmentation for a minimum of two years, it should evolve to include different clusters of purchasing power. Micro-marketing data or proxies from average housing costs are useful. Oftentimes, three to five socio-economic groups are being used.

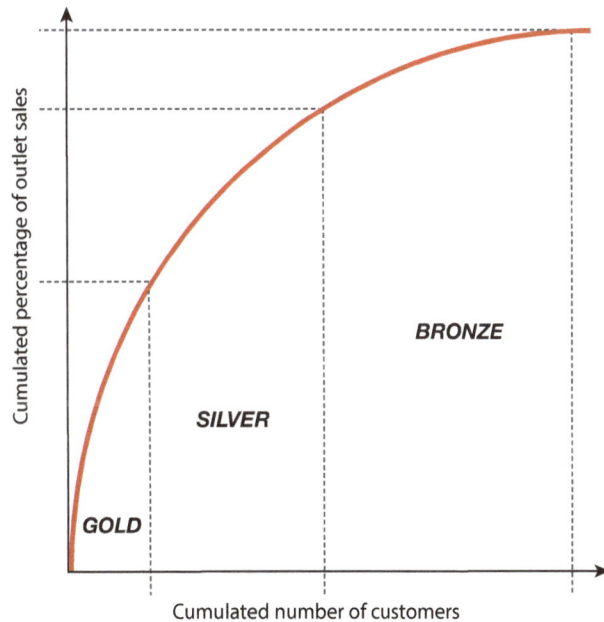

Fig. 10 — Gold / silver / bronze segmentation

EVOLVING SEGMENTATION

Segmentation in emerging markets should pass through the following stages (comp fig. 11):

Stage 1: Channel segmentation (start with three to four segments, add granularity over time);
Stage 2: Combine stage 1 with store sizes;
Stage 3: Combine stage 2 with socio-economic criteria.

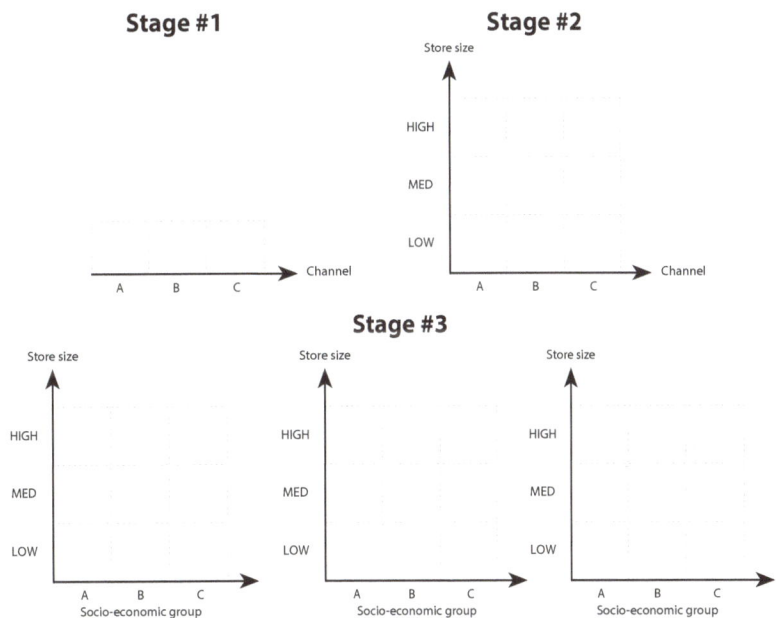

Fig. 11 — Evolving segmentation

ILLUSTRATION

The Taste Company (TTC), our fictitious ice cream manufacturer, has run an Every Dealer Survey to build a database of every potential outlet that could sell ice cream in Emergia. This survey had been outsourced to a global research company. TTC now has access to information regarding store size, store location, equipment installed, GPS coordinates, current ice cream category sales, ice cream category sales trends of the past three years and the number of shoppers entering the store per week.

During the first four years of operation in Emergia, TTC had deliberately not conducted (or pursued) any segmentation. As a result, all SKU are currently available in all channels. TTC's fifty sales people are

strictly organized by routes with each sales person visiting all outlets along his or her route.

TTC has mapped its own data with channel classifications that are being used by the local provider of syndicated data. TTC chose a segmentation of four channels:

1. Hypermarkets;
2. Small supermarkets;
3. Independent grocery stores(70% of market);
4. On premises and food service.

As a first step, TTC has decided to focus on the channel of independent grocery stores, representing 70% of industry revenue. TTC then leveraged its own data on store location and store size to add two clusters within this large channel:

Cluster 1: stores above 100 square meters, high potential, urban(35% of market);
Cluster 2: small stores, rural, lower potential, lower socio-demographic profile.

After having matched all of their stores' addresses in their database to one of these two clusters, TTC also aligned their own warehouses and distributors to follow either of those two clusters.

Next, TTC assigned its sales people to specific channels and set customer call rates depending on customer potential.

Thirdly, TTC decided that each channel requires dedicated brands to allow for targeted pricing and to avoid channel leakage (i.e. restaurant owners purchasing at hypermarkets instead of purchasing directly from TTC). The Daily brand will become exclusive for cluster 1 and 2 stores in traditional grocery."Daily" brand is supposed to have an 8% higher consumer pricing in cluster 1 after two years.

TTC's "Excellence" brand will be distributed to cluster 1 outlets and modern trade channel. The "On premise channel" will be served with exclusive service and some unique flavors of brand "excellence".

OBJECTIVES

»Being the richest man
in the cemetery doesn't
matter to me. Going
to bed at night saying
we've done something
wonderful, that's what
matters to me.«

— Steve Jobs

KEY BUSINESS INDICATORS

The previous chapter provided the foundation for setting objectives. This chapter on objectives consists of the following sub-chapters:

- Defining Key Business Indicators (KBI) on high and low level;
- Dual Planning Approach and
- Identifying and quantifying incremental growth opportunities.

The task of objective setting differs between operational and strategic plans. On the one hand, short-term planning (i.e. one-year, operational) involves objectives that are set bottom-up towards high-level KBI. On the other hand, long-term planning (i.e. three years) involves high-level KBI that are allocated top-down.

Operational plans are more granular and require more resources. Since operational plans build on strategic plans, they start with high level KBI to drill further down to a level of brand by channel. For more details on the differences between operational and strategic plans see Table 1: Short- and long-term planning elements.

	Volume	Volume Growth	Revenue	Revenue Growth	Share	Share Growth	System OI	System OI Growth
Category 1								
Category 2								
Category 3								
Category 4								
Category 5								
Category 6								
Total KO								

Fig. 12 — High-level KBI

	Volume	Volume Growth	Revenue	Revenue Growth	Distribution	Velocity	Velocity Growth	Forward Stock
SKU 1								
SKU 2								
SKU 3								
SKU 4								
SKU 5								
SKU 6								
Total SKU								

Fig. 13 — Low-level KBI

HIGH-LEVEL KBI

Below there is a list of typical high-level KBI, often stopping at the category level. (See fig. 12)

- National top-line (Net) Revenue;
- Total national volume;
- Market share by brand or category;
- National profit or EBIT.

LOW-LEVEL KBI

The potential number of low-level KBI can be very large. KBI are different from metrics (see Chapter Five) in that KBI are valid, irrelevant of the strategies or tactics being used. At the end of the Closed Commercial Loop™, KBI and metrics have to link together, utilizing the connector between chapter five and chapter one (see fig. 48)

There are standard low-level KBI that complement high-level KBI, which are likely to exist in similar ways in most FMCG companies:

- Volume (per SKU, per channel)
- Revenue (optional: gross profit) per SKU
- Distribution (weighted) by SKU
- Velocity by brand/SKU
- Forward stock (portfolio)
- Execution score

Figure 12 provides a simple tool for long-term planning that allows to set high-level KBI by category. Figure 13 is a simple table demonstrating low-level KBI on a channel level.

DUAL PLANNING APPROACH

Now that both low- and high-level KBI have been defined (i.e. value share growth of brand x in channel y), these values have to be determined and set (i.e. +2% points value share growth for brand A in channel B). This is what this section is about. Adjusting high-level KBI requires an understanding of "Strategic Growth Opportunities" (SGO), which are covered in depth in section three of this chapter.

For strategic planning, values for high-level KBI are typically created top-down only, whereas, during operational planning, values for low-level KBI are typically determined in an iterative bottom-up and top-down approach (see fig. 14).

High-level KBI values will often be received from global- or regional headquarters and are intended as corridors to leave room for local adaptation. For example: three-year revenue growth targets for each Asia market are suggested by the Asia headquarter. Each (Asia) market then breaks this number down into categories (see fig. 16).

During operational planning, when values for low-level KBIs are set, the process is iterative. It starts bottom-up and, at first, will likely fail to match with the high-level KBI. However, level synchronization is eventually achieved as a result of adjusting from high-level and low-level (see fig. 14, element 2).

Even though more demanding, the iterative approach of top-down and bottom-up ensures realistic, short-term target setting and supporting strategic objectives.

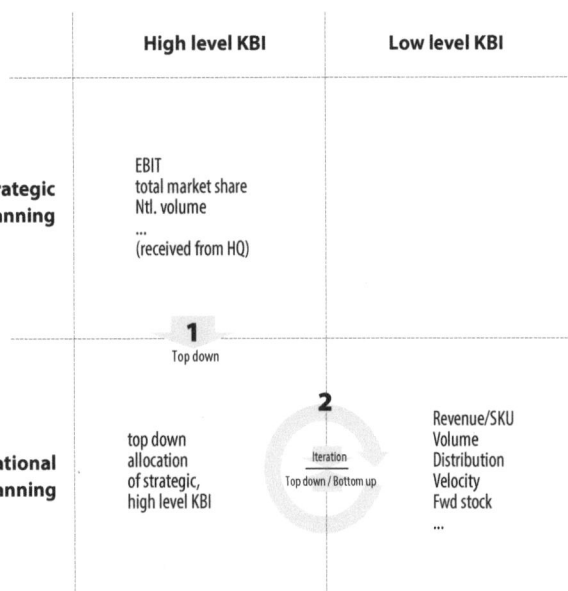

	High level KBI	Low level KBI
Strategic planning	EBIT total market share Ntl. volume ... (received from HQ)	
	1 Top down	
Operational planning	top down allocation of strategic, high level KBI	**2** Iteration Top down / Bottom up	Revenue/SKU Volume Distribution Velocity Fwd stock ...

Fig. 14 — Dual planning approach

BOTTOM-UP

For workflow see fig. 15:

1. Determine performance for each SKU x channel (or customer) using the low-level KBI (i.e. volume, revenue, share);
2. Extrapolate next period's growth based on sales history;
3. Take into account major sales impact that is to be expected or that cannot be replicated (i.e. seasonal effects, global events or legislative decisions).

This internal projection is complemented by the projected industry performance (ideally by category) by the same set of objectives. The major differences between internal projection and industry projection need to be reviewed and require a separate explanation. So far, this process should lead to targets that are safely achievable during the next period without making any major changes.

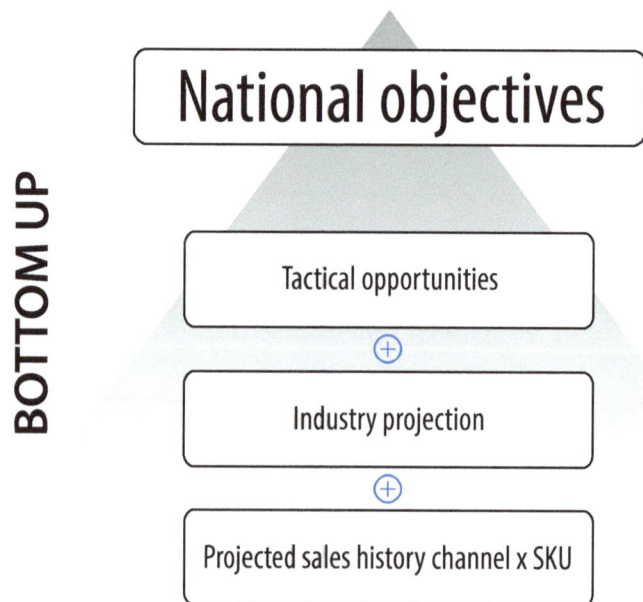

National objectives

BOTTOM UP

Tactical opportunities

⊕

Industry projection

⊕

Projected sales history channel x SKU

Fig. 15 — Bottom up

TOP-DOWN

... is a simple, yet not completely exact method (see fig. 16). For operational planning, objectives taken from the strategic plan (typically on a national level across categories) are allocated to the different segments and categories. A proven way is to allocate objectives by applying the mix of channels and categories of the past two or three years.

Though mostly done in complex spreadsheets, there is a useful tool in figure 17 to support allocation.

A typical top-down workflow to arrive at category by channel objectives:

1. Apply each national objective to channel and category by applying past mix and including assumed future industry growth;
2. Add (SGO) Strategic Growth Initiatives (i.e. Revenue Decomposition), that are covered in the following pages.

The end of this chapter presents a detailed example to further illustrate the concepts discussed above.

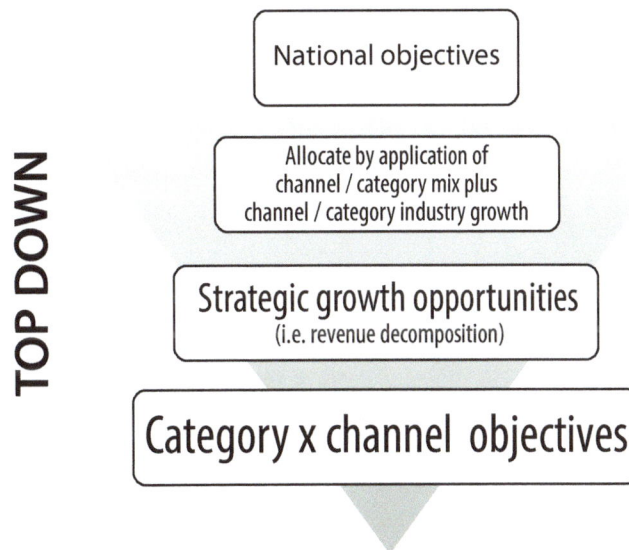

TOP DOWN

National objectives

Allocate by application of channel / category mix plus channel / category industry growth

Strategic growth opportunities
(i.e. revenue decomposition)

Category x channel objectives

Fig. 16 — Top down

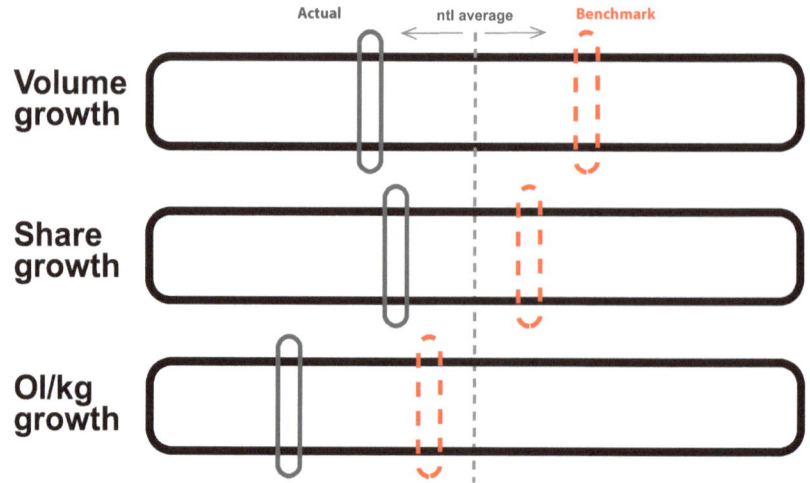

Fig. 17 — Directional top down objectives

Figure 17 illustrates how three high-level KBI are being allocated to one of the channels. The dotted gray line indicates the national target. Gray and red boxes show actual and planned KBI for this channel.

NOTE

In a real life planning situation, there will be instances where a channel target will differ significantly from its current trend: mostly driven by assumptions made based on macro drivers, key product launchers, expanded distribution and so on. Any assumption has to be properly documented in order to avoid double counting.

IDENTIFYING STRATEGIC GROWTH OPPORTUNITIES (SGO)

In order to adjust high-level KBI to actual channel or category targets, historic data and market trends are insufficient to determine the full growth potential.

This book introduces two tools that will help to identify and quantify Strategic Growth Opportunities (SGO):

1. Revenue decomposition and
2. New versus existing shoppers.

Both tools serve the same purpose and have similar output, but they are different in their complexity and user-friendliness. Both tools work on a default level of category by channel. The following two sections will give a detailed description of each tool.

SGO TOOL NUMBER ONE: REVENUE DECOMPOSITION

The first SGO tool helps to quantify the potential of a given combination of category by channel through decomposing the revenue into the following four drivers (see fig. 18):

- Population (number of shoppers in a given universe);
- Capture rate (or purchase incidence);
- Frequency (how often do shoppers purchase);
- Basket size (average amount spend per purchase).

If multiplied, these four drivers will always lead to the total revenue of the assumed universe. For more information, see an example calculation at the end of this chapter.

Before discussing these four levers of revenue decomposition in more detail, the opportunities around the P-lever for Population need to be canceled out.

Consumer goods manufacturers can neither impact a population nor can they realistically impact the number of shoppers visiting a customer.

Retailers often perform deep price cuts on top brands in order to recruit new shoppers for their outlet. For manufacturers, this proactively bears a risk for long-term price deterioration and price wars among retailers.

	Channel 1	Channel 2	Channel 3	Best in class
Incidence				
Transaction				
Amount (volume)				
Amount ($/liter)				

Fig. 18 — Revenue decomposition

INCIDENCE

Incidence (also known as capture or closure rate) describes how many shoppers visiting an outlet actually purchase the chosen category. Consumer goods manufacturers usually consider four weeks an adequate time period to define capture rate.

TRANSACTION

Transaction (or frequency) measures the number of purchase transactions of shoppers per period. Typical classifications of frequency metrics would be daily, daily +, weekly, or weekly +.

AMOUNT

Amount (also known as basket size – in value) should be further decomposed into the volume being purchased and the consumer price per volume unit (i.e. $/kg).

These three metrics are now complemented by a best in class benchmark, so that the potential headroom can be calculated for each driver.

Best in class benchmark may include:

- Performance of the same category in a different channel;
- Performance of a different brand and/or category in the same channel;
- Total category or a specific competitor in the same channel.

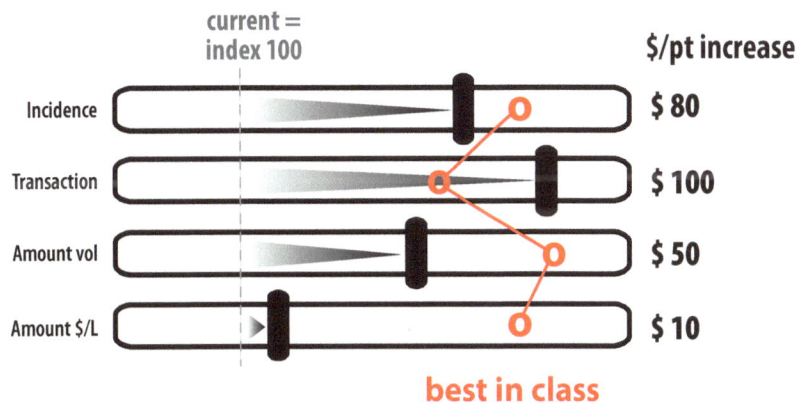

Fig. 19 — Revenue decomposition sliders

BENCHMARKING

Once current performance for each driver has been determined, it is easy to calculate the revenue impact for each index point of increase.

In fig. 19 the largest revenue opportunity lies in Transaction, with $100 per index point increase. In this example, the future transaction is planned to exceed the current best in class example.

The second most impactful driver is the incidence with $80 per index point. Volume amount is the third most impactful driver, while revenue per volume unit has the least impact on total revenue.

A company would chose a driver depending on where the gap to the benchmark is largest, as this delivers the highest leverage.

CUSTOMER APPLICATION

The above approach of decomposing revenue drivers is often used to create winning plans with large retail customers: best players identify the customer objectives and map them against the revenue drivers.

What makes the Revenue Decomposition Tool so compelling is that it quantifies the opportunity. It describes the WHAT, but, at the same time, it only gives small clues on HOW to achieve this.

This is the role of the 4A Tool. The chapter on tactics will come back to this topic and discuss revenue drivers, linking them to specific actions.

SGO TOOL NUMBER TWO: NEW VERSUS EXISTING SHOPPERS

New versus existing shoppers is the second SGO tool to identify and quantify strategic growth opportunities. Whereas the first tool decomposes revenue (optional volume) into incidence, transaction and amount, this tool groups a total of ten drivers into two categories: revenue coming from existing shoppers versus revenue coming from new shoppers. See fig. 20 for a tree-like structure.

In addition to these ten drivers, the impact of improved mix, which is derived either from brand-, pack- or channel-mix, must be considered. However, changing the mix significantly is only feasible in very specific situations, which is why this book will not discuss this topic in more depth. The group of new consumers includes four growth drivers, while the group of existing consumers includes an additional six drivers. Quantifying growth opportunity requires us to understand the correlation between each of the ten drivers and revenue, as illustrated below for four growth drivers.

Driver 1: Brand equity scores or media GDP correlation to revenue uplift;

Driver 2: Correlation of POS investments (i.e. displays, signage...) to same store sales;

Driver 3: Additional consumption occasions: what is the potential size of this new occasion if our brand can take the same share as in existing occasions?

Driver 4: Reaching new consumers with enlarged portfolio: what is the potential size, assuming the company can achieve a certain share?

Potential drivers of incremental revenue can be found in the tree-like structure displayed in figure 20.

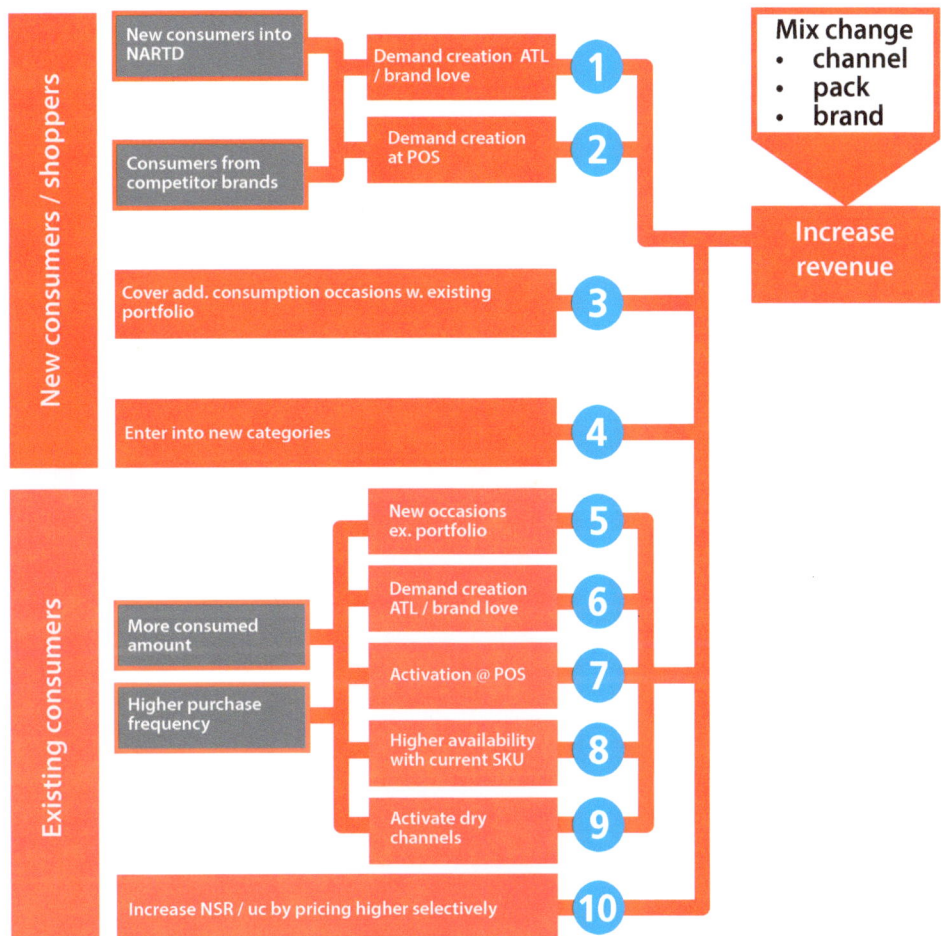

Fig. 20 — New vs. existing shoppers

Drivers are grouped into growth coming from

- Existing shoppers or consumers (i.e. vertical growth) or
- New shoppers (horizontal).

Unsurprisingly, the number of individual growth drivers is large and, in reality, drivers overlap. Unlike the Revenue Decomposition Tool, this tool does not offer benchmarking.

PRIORITIZING INCREMENTAL GROWTH OPPORTUNITIES

Irrelevant of whether the Revenue Decomposition Tool or the New versus Existing tool is being used, multiple opportunities will emerge that require prioritization. A proven tool for a first prioritization of multiple growth opportunities is displayed in figure 21. The graph displays the relationship between relative feasibility (i.e. production capacity, sales force capabilities, required investment and so forth) and relative business impact (that is, the performance of growth opportunities among each other in terms of expected volume, revenue and profit).

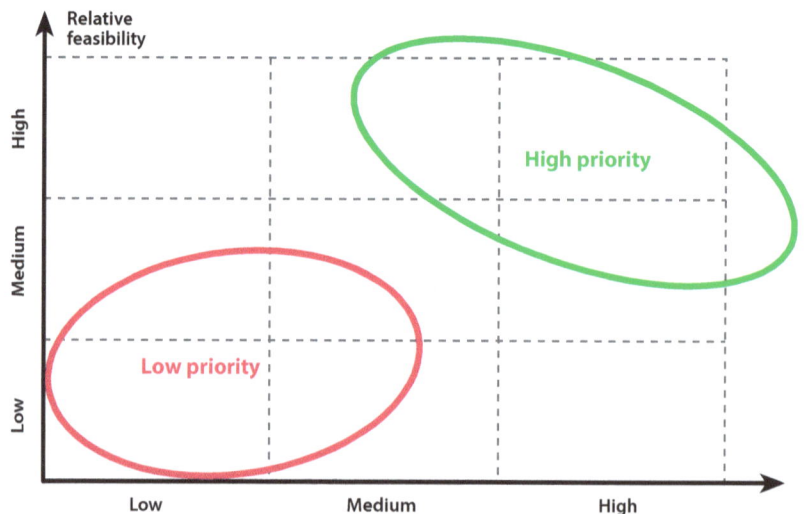

Fig. 21 — Strategic priorization matrix

ILLUSTRATION

For its operational commercial plan, TTC created objectives for cluster 1 (traditional grocery channel, large, urban, higher income) by cascading down its national objectives .

TTC, Emergia, was given the following high-level KBI from the regional headquarter:

- +5% annual volume growth,
- +7% annual growth operating profit,
- +1.5% revenue share growth per annum.

SETTING HIGH-LEVEL KBI

Instead of applying the national growth rate of volume and revenue equally to all channels and categories, TTC used the top-down approach by looking at historic natural growth rates and added strategic growth opportunities (SGO) to cascade the national targets down to channels and categories.

In the past year, cluster 1's revenue growth rate was at 2.5% cycling strong growth, a little behind the industry growth and certainly not at the required 7% for next year. At the same time, the modern trade channels, due to strong outlet growth, have been growing at 5%.

Therefore, next year's natural growth for cluster 1 was set at +4%

When TTC identified SGO by using the Revenue Decomposition tool, they determined that increasing purchase incidence (with new users) and improving the consumption frequency with loyal users could yield them additional 3% growth. This growth would have to be fueled by stronger in-store activation and its execution.

4% natural growth plus 3% of untapped SGO led to a full year revenue growth target of 7%.

The same process was applied to cluster 2 and the other channels in Emergia. All plans consolidated will link to the national revenue growth target of 7%.

SETTING LOW-LEVEL KBI

With a channel target in place, TTC now started to use the iterative bottom-up and top-down approach for their key SKU. TTC started with their Daily brand 1L chocolate pack in traditional grocery.

TTC's brand manager projected current sales trend to be +3% — assuming same price increase as last year.

One additional percent point of growth is planned from increased distribution. One percent point from velocity increase (doubling the number of facings of the 1L pack). Additional 0.5% growth from improved instore execution. Together this adds up to +5.5% growth, which is beyond the estimated industry growth.

While working on the growth rates of their seven key packs that represent 70% of TTC's revenue, TTC continuously monitored the consolidated growth rate and the variance to the 7% target for this channel. By changing and adapting some of the growth drivers, such as number and depth of planned price offs, or the planned change of forward stock, all packs combined led to the required level coming from high-level KBI.

STRATEGIES

»The essence of strategy
is choosing what not to
do.«

—Michael Porter

Now that the previous chapter has determined strategic growth opportunities and objectives, this chapter fully develops these strategies by using the following steps:

- Building a channel profile;
- Designing the growth strategy to support SGO;
- Creating or reviewing pricing and sizing;
- Building the activation blueprint (or floor plan);
- Creating or reviewing the execution tracking model;
- Creating or reviewing the customer service model.

Definition: The term "strategy" describes a bundle of high-level actions that all point into the same direction and have the purpose of bringing previously determined objectives to life and allocating resources effectively and efficiently.

CHANNEL PROFILING

THE OBJECTIVE OF PROFILING

The objective of profiling is to determine similarities and differences between channels when it comes to addressing customers, shoppers and consumers commercially.

The role of a segment (or channel) is constructed out of three profiles and strategic opportunities:

- Shopper profile;
- Consumer profile;
- Customer profile.
- Strategic Growth Opportunities

All good commercial strategies are based on a thoughtful description of current and future behavior of key stakeholders: customers, consumers and shoppers. However, many plans have ignored the perspective of customers and shoppers.

Whereas consumer needs are naturally included in all good marketing programs, experience has shown that far too often associates in commercial roles fail to add customer and shopper profiles early on in the planning process.

Failing to include these at this stage will result in inefficiencies when planning tactics for retailers.

Designing profiles has strong similarities to planning a customer call. If a win-win solution is the destination, it is likely to become a successful plan.

BENEFITS OF CHANNEL PROFILES

Channel strategies that build on profiles will proof to be more successful when it comes to persuading trade partners, inspiring sales teams and deriving executable actions.

Manufacturers, who support their channel strategies with strong shopper, consumer and customer insights, face less risk of retailers rejecting suggested initiatives.

Customer strategies that are based on the respective channel and include strong insights are easier to agree on. In fact, they help build a collaborative, trustful and lasting relationship, because insights shared with customers are considered to be a non-financial service that builds trust and long lasting relationships. Being a non-financial support, services and insights also help reduce the annual pressure on terms and conditions.

SHOPPER PROFILES

Shopper profiles describe current behavior, needs and wants of shoppers and consumers.

The list below is designed to help build a shopper profile (by channel):

1. Top two consumption occasions a purchase is made for;
2. Type of consumption occasion: immediate, imminent or for future consumption;

NOTE

Comparing profiles across different channels is highly recommended!

3. Shopping mission – i.e. unplanned fill in, impulse, planned stock up trip, urgent item;
4. Shopper socio-demographics;
5. Visit frequency;
6. Visit duration;
7. Average basket size and relation between basket size and disposable income;
8. Basket composition and correlation with other food items;
9. Means to get to the store (by foot, car or public transportation);
10. Average volume (pack size) purchase;
11. Time of day for visit.

As the concept of "shoppers" may still be relatively new to some companies, many companies have already started to build insights and to strengthen awareness of shoppers through shop-alongs or shopper interviews. In fact, some FMCG companies have created avatars in order to bring the typical shopper to life and study his behavior. See fig. 22 for a graphical combination of a consumer and a shopper profile.

Shopper profile

On the go
Male, 25-35 caucasian
Looks for convenience

| | Occasion | Mission | Income | Gender | Region | Ethnic |

Fig. 22 — Shopper profile

CONSUMER PROFILES

As most of the existing marketing literature covers consumers very well, the discussion of this topic will be kept very brief in this book.

Consumer profiles are typically built using:

- Socio-demographics;
- Need states (i.e. the underlying motivation to consume);
- Consumption patterns and consumption occasions;
- Social clusters describing how and with whom they spend their time.

CUSTOMER PROFILE

The following questions are designed to help build a customer profile:

- Number of outlets;
- Source of growth
- Differentiating factors versus competitors — the unique proposition of this customer addressing shoppers;

- Primary growth drivers, i.e. horizontal or vertical, mergers and acquisitions ...;
- Set of closest competitors;
- Personal motivation and needs of the key decision makers (often as important as the customer's strategy).

See fig. 23 for a simple table format channel role, which consolidates shopper, consumer and customer profiles and strategic growth opportunities (from the previous chapter).

	Channel 1	Channel 2	Channel 3
Business objective			
SGO			
Occasion			
Shopping mission			
Primary audience			
Primary category			
Primary brand			
Primary pack size			

Fig. 23 — Channel role

DESIGNING A GROWTH STRATEGY

By now, all components describing the WHAT have been compiled. These are:

- Objectives;
- Strategic Growth Opportunities (SGO);
- Channel role.

With this information in place, a proven way to develop the HOW (i.e. the strategy), which has been used in different variations in various FMCG companies, is to group growth strategies into four tiers. We will call this the 4A Tool (see fig. 24):

- **Affordability**: Answers the question whether the product is available at low enough price points to allow for maximum penetration of the potential user base;
- **Availability**: The distribution level of a product or service;
- **Activation**: Degree of commercial support given to a product, such as secondary placements, permanent messaging in store and promotion;
- **Accuracy** (or degree of segmentation): Level of precision used to market a product to the various shopper or consumer segments.

The 4A Tool complements the Revenue Decomposition Tool. The 4A Tool strongly emphasizes the HOW, whereas the Revenue Decomposition Tool reveals WHAT can be improved without articulating the required strategy.

Yet simpler, the 4A strategies (see fig. 24) can be labeled as either horizontal or vertical growth strategies. Horizontal growth results from expansion, meaning that either more outlets are being served or that a higher number of items is available in existing distribution. In contrast, vertical growth refers to growth derived from stronger same store sales within existing distribution.

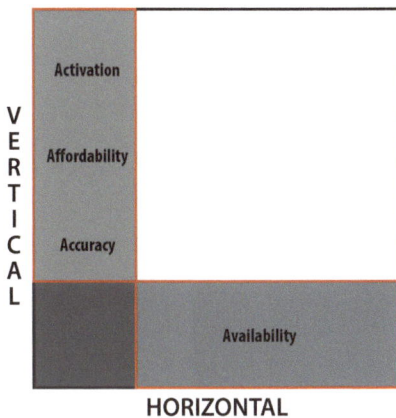

Fig. 24 — 4A TOOL; horizontal / vertical

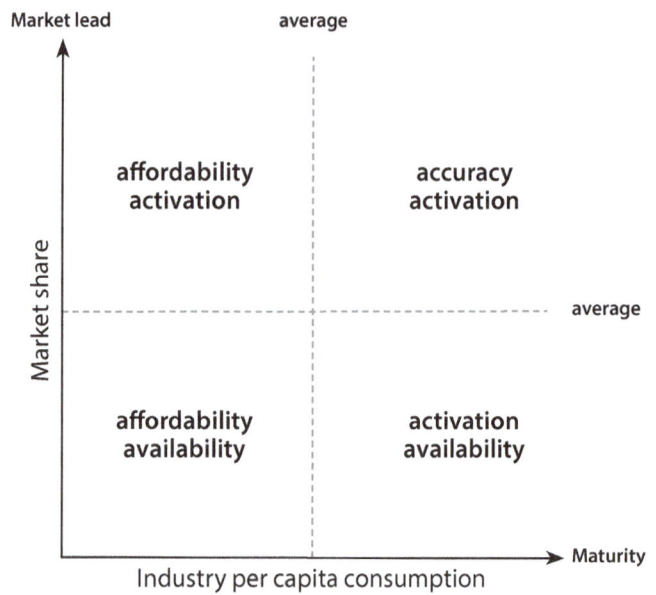

Fig. 25 — 4A selection matrix

DEFINITION AND MIX OF 4A STRATEGIES

To determine the mix of the two 4A strategies, let us now take a closer look at the two-by-two matrix outlined in fig. 25.

HORIZONTAL

The x-axis (or horizontal axis) measures the degree of maturity (or the level of saturation) of the given category. Global manufacturers apply per capita consumption benchmarks to this axis.

VERTICAL

The vertical y-axis describes the competitive situation of a specific company's category in this channel. Volume or revenue market share works best as an indicator.

LOWER LEFT CORNER

In a situation of low maturity and low competitiveness, the number one strategy for this category in this channel is affordability. The number two strategy is availability.

What this means is that in a market, where per capita consumption and shares are low, this category has to be expanded. In an environment of developing and emerging markets, pricing and sizing of products to make them affordable on a daily basis is the key to success. For example, over the past ten years there has been a large number of food and beverage items, which have been downsized, and thus down priced, to reach a wider consumer base in such a situation.

AFFORDABILITY

Affordability refers to pack sizes and every day availability, as opposed to sampling. However, sampling can also be considered as a temporary tactic to expand a consumer based category.

AVAILABILITY

Availability means distributing products and having them available for the consumer. This strategy can focus either on expanding horizontal or vertical distribution.

UPPER LEFT CORNER

This corner describes a situation, in which there is low maturity combined with a strong competition. In this case, the commercial strategy mix will shift to pricing and in-store performance.

Given the small size of this category and its large opportunities for growth, affordability will remain the top priority. Activation now, carried out from a strong, advantageous position, will support category expansion and help defend a leadership position.

UPPER RIGHT CORNER

Market leadership in an almost saturated category calls for accuracy and activation.

ACCURACY

Accuracy, also known as differentiation, is the art of targeting consumer and shopper needs with precision. This strategy is pursued in order to leverage the fact that there exist different consumption locations and shopping missions within a single channel. Different shopper types allow for differentiated pricing, which in turn helps to extract value and grow revenue.

A company, which chooses accuracy to be their strategy in a specific category within a specific channel, should, at this point, consider reviewing their segmentation in the market. This is to double-check that the level of granularity, which they are applying to their current planning, reflects the maximum accuracy or precision that this company can afford. Maximum: highest level of planning sophistication a company can actually execute.

LOWER RIGHT CORNER

The lower right corner is labeled: High maturity of the category in combination with a low competitive position. There exists sufficient consumption, yet somebody else leads the market. In that situation, activation and availability are the two most profitable commercial strategies. Activation will help to convert shoppers into buyers of the respective brand at the point of purchase. This needs to happen at a maximum amount of outlets in this channel.

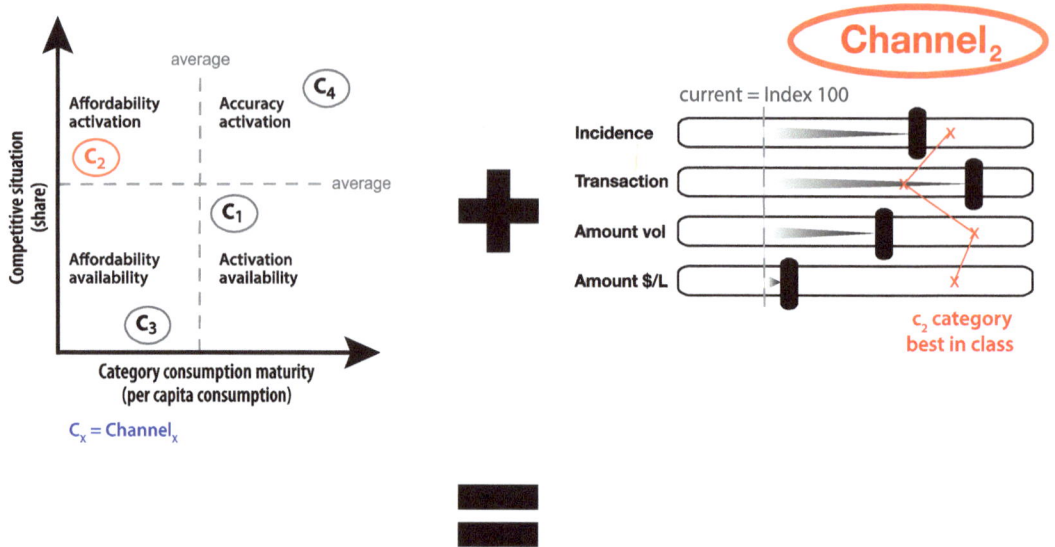

Fig. 26 — Combination 4A tool and Revenue Decomposition Tool

Incidence through improved affordability
Affordability will help number of transactions, yet reduce price per liter.
Activation to support growth of transactions, less focus on volume / transaction or price per liter.

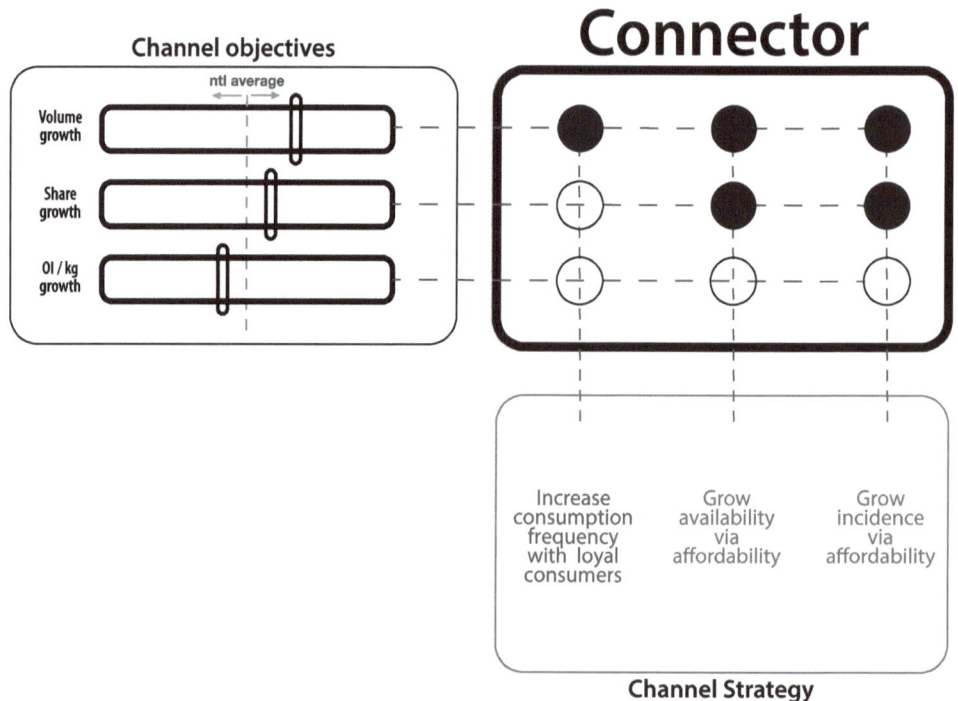

Fig. 27 — Connector

FINE-TUNING THE STRATEGY

Now that SGO have determined the WHAT of the strategy and the 4A Tool has revealed the HOW, both need to be merged. The steps are as follows:

1. Select 4A Tool and choose the relevant quadrant in the two-by-two matrix(see fig. 25);
2. Select primary revenue decomposition drivers (see fig. 19: Revenue decomposition sliders);
3. Overlay both choices (see fig. 26);
4. Articulate the strategy (by category and by channel).

Figure 26 provides an example of the merging process for channel two (C2 = upper left corner).

The 4A Tool calls for affordability and activation for channel two. The Revenue Decomposition Tool calls for a disproportionately high focus on incidence and transactions. Combining both tools creates the strategy for channel two.

Finally, it is time to add this new channel strategy to the channel role, which was developed earlier in this chapter (see fig. 23).

CONNECTORS

Each chapter is linked to the following chapter by means of connectors. This helps to keep the content connected and to create a Closed Commercial Loop™. To work towards the commercial loop (and the Hoshin-Kanri Matrix, i.e. the final tracking tool of the planning process) upstream and downstream visual connectors are created at the end of each chapter. Figure 27 illustrates how three (channel-) objectives are being connected to the (channel-) strategy. The filled dots indicate a match, whereas the blank dots indicate no match.

For this chapter, the determined strategies are graphically connected upstream to the channel objectives (from the previous chapter) and downstream to the next chapter on tactics. These connectors reveal immediately if objectives are not being supported by strategies or if strategies have been developed that do not directly link back to the channel objectives.

CREATING / REVIEWING PRICING AND SIZING

Assortment and pricing are perhaps the most critical elements of commercial strategies.

Assortment and pricing build on 4A strategies and SGO that have been determined in previous chapters.

Depending on the frequency of changes, "assortment and pricing" theoretically have the potential to also become a tactical tool.

SIX-STEPS WORKFLOW

1. Assess current pack and price architecture;
2. Create category price line;
3. Map velocity ratio and gross profit;
4. Consolidate;
5. Prioritize best performing pack price bundles and merge them into a new architecture;
6. Quantify business impact.

STEP 1: ASSESS CURRENT PACK AND PRICE ARCHITECTURE

In order to review packaging and pricing architectures, one must scrutinize them from the following perspectives (see fig. 28):

- Shopper needs and strategic package function;
- Competitiveness and profitability;
- Current pricing and share performance in the market.

Even though the sequence of the upcoming analytics in regards to these perspectives is eventually irrelevant, experience has shown that starting from shopper needs and combining these with packaging functions is the best starting point.

1
*Strategic function
x shopper needs*

*Assortment
&
Pricing*

3
*Price points
x share*

2
*Competitiveness
x Protability*

Fig. 28 — Sweetspot

SHOPPER AND CONSUMER NEEDS – CONSUMPTION OCCASIONS

To optimize the current architecture, it is critical to understand why, how and when a shopper chooses certain pack sizes or price points. Labeling existing SKUs with the primary shopper need requires shopper data or a deep understanding of consumption patterns within a trade channel.

STRATEGIC PACKAGING FUNCTIONS

Consumer needs – consumption occasions – describe the first dimension, the strategic function of this packaging represents the second dimension. The matrix maps occasions (horizontal) with pack functions (vertical) – see fig. 29.

Packaging functions describe the job of a certain pack, i.e. the role that it has to play to meet strategic and competitive objectives within the total portfolio. Consider packaging functions to be similar to the concept of soccer positions: Defense, forward, and midfield ...

Even though the terminology across FMCG companies varies, three basic packaging functions can be applied across multiple industries:

- Cash outlay function (also known as Budget-function);
- Value function (also known as fighter packs);
- Upgrade function.

	on premise	at home	
	Immediate	Imminent	Delayed
Cash outlay			
Value		pack $ / UNIT MIX	
Upgrade			

Fig. 29 — Assortment matrix

CASH OUTLAY FUNCTION

The cash outlay function helps a company to attract consumers on a budget. For example, low-income groups in emerging markets that are restricted by the amount of cash they carry with them. The objective is to grow this consumer base either by expanding the total category or by converting users from competition. This is done by addressing a low cash outlay with low absolute price points.

Packaging according to the cash outlay function typically has the lowest absolute price point within the portfolio, but not necessarily the lowest price per unit.

Such packs will therefore be either small sized packs, packs with less convenience or packs that are less attractive due to higher costs.

Cash outlay packs enable manufacturers to offer recruitment items at a very attractive, low consumer price and to minimize profitability losses, which are likely to occur as a result of cannibalization triggered by the low price point.

Typical examples for budget function packs would be:

- Miniature whiskey bottles;
- Hair and beauty products for one or two applications.

VALUE FUNCTION

All branded CPG manufacturers need to grow and protect their sales volume share. Value packs (also known as fighter packs) address existing loyal consumers by offering them price discounts, when purchasing a larger quantity opposed to the average quantity shopped. A value pack has a lower price per unit than the average pack within the packaging portfolio.

By lowering the price per unit, which typically is done by means of extra-large packs, multi-packs or overfill-packs, consumers are incentivized to stock up on more volume at home. Availability then leads to increased consumption in the same period of time.

In the case of branded consumer goods, many price wars are fought over such value function packs. Value packs may be available for promotions or specific seasons only. For example, think of large confectionery stock up packs prior to Easter or Ramadan season. However, they may also be available permanently in appropriate channels, such as cash and carry formats, or hypermarkets, where stocking up is the prevailing shopping mission.

UPGRADE FUNCTION

The upgrade function seeks to drive revenue growth rather than volume growth. Any CPG company will find certain clusters in emerging or developing markets. This allows them to increase the price per unit substantially by offering the same or similar product quality, but in a packaging that is either highly attractive, highly convenient, or provides added consumer value for other reasons.

In the beer industry, there are examples of products sold in aluminum packaging that have been created by globally renowned designers. These products are sold at 300% the price of the regular product on a per liter basis. Example: Heineken (QR 21)

In the confectionery industry, high quality, small luxurious packaging exists, allowing a host to put this exclusive packaging on the dinner table with friends. Example: Ferrero (QR 22)

Veuve Cliquot offered a luxurious secondary packaging, which served as a gift box, as well as an attractive, ready-to-use ice cooler, to enhance the product experience even further. For images see site (QR 23)

These consumer benefits created through packaging, not product quality, make it possible to increase price per unit, retailer profit and manufacturer profit. Upgraded packs extract excess spending power from consumers. From a portfolio perspective, upgraded packaging offsets the lower profits per unit generated by value packs. While the volume contribution of value packs may go up to 60% of total sales, upgrade packs will typically contribute only 10% to 20% of total volume. Upgraded packs, which are sold at 200% above the average price per unit, offset soft margins of value packs.

Like value packs, upgraded packs are typically limited to specific segments of a market: demographics with higher socio-economic profiles and lower price elasticity, higher priced channels, such as large international hypermarkets, and captive locations, such as upscale bars, international hotels and fine dining restaurants. As food service does not have secondary packaging, the pack itself must be the hero pack.

Figure 29 displays how to map existing SKUs in this matrix of packaging functions and consumer needs. Assuming three basic functions plus three basic needs, this matrix will be able to hold and map all current packs.

Each of those nine quadrants will contain additional information, such as pack size, pack format, price per unit and percentage mix. Depending on the market, channel and category, either all or only selected quadrants need to be filled.

ILLUSTRATION

The following are three potential consumption occasions for our TTC ice-cream brand:

- Immediate craving,
- Watching TV and
- Meals at home.

Depending on the consumption occasion, consumption will take place immediately on premise or somewhat delayed at home. In some industries, SKUs first have to be grouped into functions or flavors before being labeled with occasions. Examples: breakfast tea, infusion, health related products. In a different category, say alcoholic spirits, it may make sense to look across multiple flavors to understand the driver of consumption. In the case of spirits, consumption occasions for multiple flavors could be: party with friends, digest after a heavy meal, wine down alone, etc. Experience has shown that grouping SKUs by primary consumption occasion helps to determine the appropriate in-store messaging. Grouping by shopping missions links nicely to specific channels (stock up trip equals large store). However, this method is incapable of addressing the underlying consumer needs to convert shoppers into buyers.

STEP 2: UTILIZING THE PRICE LINE TOOL
TO DETERMINE PRICE POINT GAPS

In the previous step, some indications to price points were given:

Budget packs need to have the absolute lowest price point in each of the different consumption situations. Value packs need to have the lowest price per unit in each of the consumption occasions and upgrade function packs should have the highest price per unit.

With help of the Price Line Tool (see fig. 30), price points from competitors in the same category, as well as from competitors outside of the respective category, will now be included.

This is required, since categories compete against each other for the same consumption occasion. The price line shows all local price points horizontally.

VERTICALLY

The vertical axis displays volume or revenue share for each industry and for each specific brand. This graphic should display all competitors, own brands and known category competitors.

HORIZONTALLY

Looking horizontally will help us to identify price points that are currently not covered. In addition, the horizontal axis highlights the relative importance (i.e. the share) of each price point in the industry. For this, it helps to group multiple price points together.

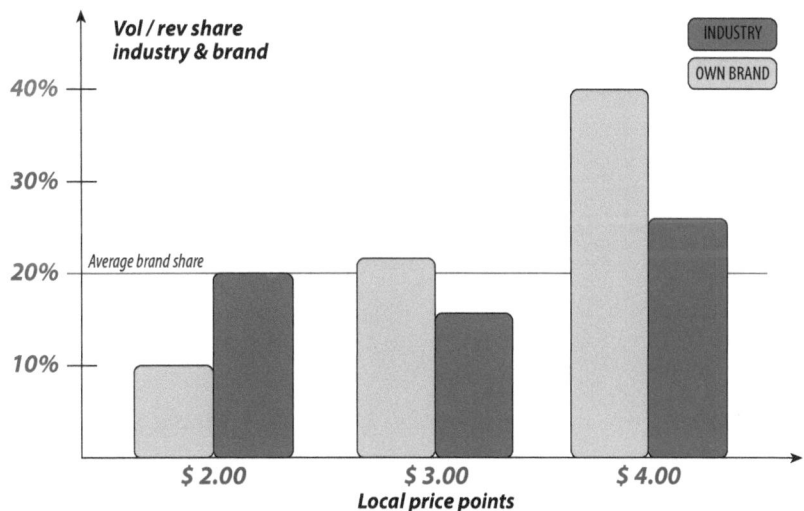

Fig. 30 — Price line

The manufacturer should now benchmark whether a fair share in all major price point clusters has been achieved. In each of the price clusters, share is equivalent to the total market share.

MAGIC PRICE POINTS

The second consideration when investigating price points is to understand whether a category has so-called magic price points or thresholds that must not be exceeded. Magic price points play an important role in order to nourish and grow consumer recruitment, thus creating a constant or growing consumer base. Affordability for the top audience is a key consideration for FMCG companies.

In particular when looking at packs with a budget function, every local market has its own magic price point, which is driven by coinage increments, disposable income and price gaps versus competition. The consumer base grows if the magic price point is continuously monitored, if cash outlay is accounted for and if the absolute price point requires one, at most two, local coins or bills.

NOTE

It is the expected incremental profit RELATIVE (to the other ideas), not absolute versus existing products.

STEP 3: VELOCITY RATIO VERSUS COMPETITION

The third assessment will help to identify those products or packaging that have a competitive advantage compared to its competitors.

By calculating a ratio of velocity versus its competitors (rate of sale own brand versus rate of sale competition) the strongest packs can easily be determined.

The velocity ratio is now cross-tabbed with the gross profit per unit of the manufacturer (see fig. 31).

It is suggested that one complements this small tool with a graphic analysis, as displayed in figure 32: (vertical) availability, share of shelf for packs and retail margin are compared against competition.

STEP 4: CONSOLIDATE

From the previous three assessments various opportunities for changes in size and price points have emerged. Based on these insights and analyses, these new configurations better address shopper needs, stra-

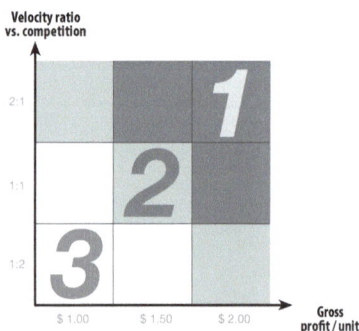

Fig. 31 — ROS OI

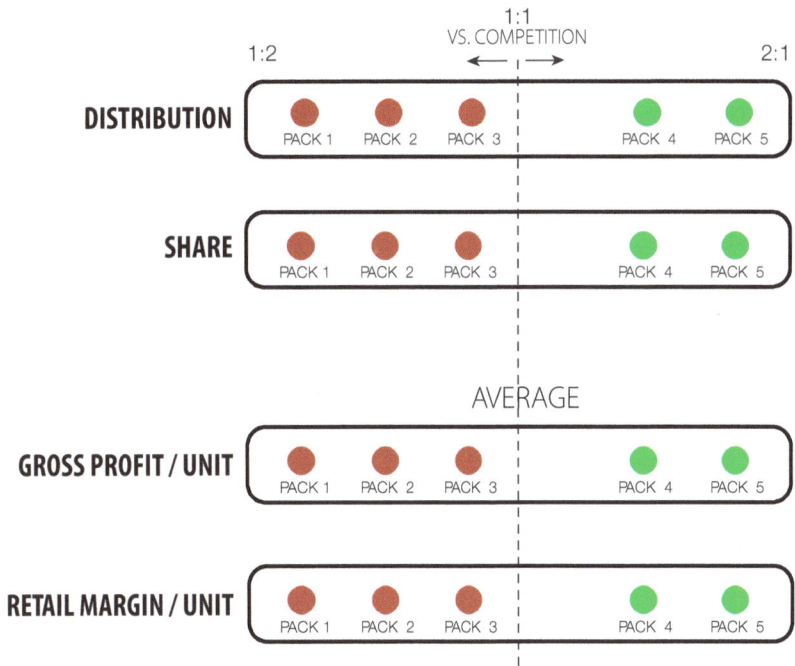

Fig. 32 — SKU performance

tegic intent, competitor environment, and profitability requirements compared to the current architecture.

The consolidation step is pulling all changes together. This is achieved by means of creating an updated matrix of packaging functions multiplied by consumption occasions.

STEP 5: PRIORITIZE PACK / PRICE SUGGESTIONS

Oftentimes, the number of pack/price initiatives is high. Therefore, a filter has to be applied in order to shortlist initiatives before further evaluation and quantitative research will shortlist them even further. See fig. 33 for a simple way of ranking pack/ price ideas.

The horizontal axis shows the expected incremental profit triggered by the change. Horizontally, each pack/price proposal receives a label on potential investments that are required to produce and bring these proposals to market. Think of investments into new production lines, new packaging, more sales force resources, and include all other cost implications resulting from this solution.

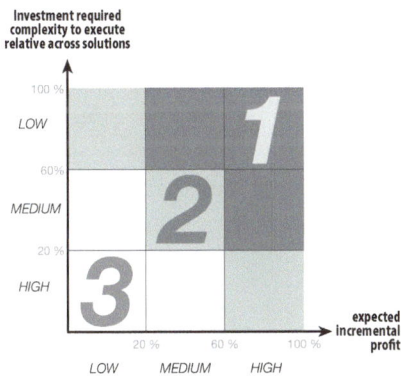

Fig. 33 — Investment x profit filter

STEP 6: VALIDATION

Validation of newly generated ideas for packaging and pricing can be resource intensive. Depending on the degree of innovation and the number of scenarios and channels, validation may take several months and require massive investments into research.

To arrive at reliable, quantitative data, CPG companies typically use either price elasticity modeling and/or conjoint analysis. Price elasticity studies are fast and cost effective. However, in absence of scan data in a traditional grocery environment, this tool is difficult to carry out.

Conjoint analysis is more complex and requires more resources. Both methodologies have delivered reliable results for many years across multiple categories. As conjoint analysis and elasticity modeling both are well-documented disciplines in economic literature, this book will not go into any more detail regarding these research methodologies.

In some markets, however, field-testing may be an option to precede quantitative research. Field-testing can be set up fast and cost effectively. Directional results can be expected even from a relatively small number of test and control stores. In some markets, this may be sufficient, while, in other markets, field-testing may serve as a way to shortlist the number of potential solutions to be tested and modeled.

PORTFOLIO VIEW, NOT SKU VIEW

Once the modeling has delivered expected volume changes by SKU, it is up to finance specialists to generate new value chains (profit/loss statements). It is important to note that contrasting current and future scenarios should always happen on a portfolio level. Coming back to the concept of packaging functions being similar to positions in a soccer team, all packaging and pricing recommendations perform together as a team. Hence, their impact should also be evaluated as a team.

Comparing profitability of two individual SKUs (current and proposed) does not allow us to measure the impact of the total portfolio or packaging team. Therefore, this approach is shortsighted.

As all processes and tools in this book, the described process works best on the level of one category (or brand) and within one execution segment (i.e. trade channel). Consequently, this process may have to be repeated as many times as the number of categories multiplied by the number of channels.

MUST PLACE ITEMS

Once all categories/brands within one channel have been reviewed, all new pack sizes and price points need to be merged into one document per execution segment/channel.

We call this document the "Must place item list." This list represents the orchestra or bundle of core items that have to be made available together. As with a symphony orchestra, it takes all items to perform, not just some.

Oftentimes, companies have gone through a phase of SKU proliferation before they start thinking about "must place items." Hence, discontinuation of specific SKU in certain channels will be required, since shelf space is limited.

Determining the list of must place items can either take place at this point in the process, or shortly before creating the planograms during the blueprint creation.

This book will cover the "must place item list" in the next chapter, which explains how to create the activation blueprint.

BUILDING THE ACTIVATION BLUEPRINT

The activation blueprint, also known as floor plan or POP plan or look of success, is the consolidation and the final product of multiple commercial planning elements.

A floor plan summarizes numerically and graphically all permanent and temporary in-store activities of a company. Floor plans are built from the bottom up, starting with the lowest level of segmentation that is being executed.

Three distinct floor plans are required if a company has decided to segment their market into three trade channels.

OBJECTIVE OF A FLOOR PLAN

- Summarize and consolidate all activities at the Point of Purchase;
- Display required actions for easy implementation;
- Provide win-win rationale for customers.

Floor planning provides the foundation for many important commercial work streams:

- Plan in-store marketing budgets;
- Plan execution tracking;
- Potential changes in the way that a company serves its customers.

Going through the following short process helps to match, prioritize and align all individual elements (coming from separate planning work, such as assortment, sales equipment and in-store communication).

The floor plan maps all elements into a single, comprehensive plan and, in addition, links all elements to specific geographical zones of a new retail outlet.

FLOOR-PLANNING WORKFLOW

- Pre-work;
- Map inventory with zones;
- Permanent messaging;
- Visible inventory;
- Planograms;
- Equipment;
- Budgeting;
- Creation of floor plan;
- Customer value proposition;
- Pilot;
- Train sales force.

1 – PRE-WORK TASKS

- Familiarize yourself with channel roles and channel objectives;
- Create "must place items list" (cf.);
- Add in-store materials, which are currently in use, and complete the inventory list with other materials suited.

Divide this inventory list into four subgroups:

- In-store communication;
- In-store merchandising;
- Sales equipment;
- Must place items.

Now, start to map shopper profile with the inventory list in order to understand which of the general characteristics and which items from the inventory can address opportunities.

Ensure that access is provided to a representative layout of a retail environment (floor plan, blueprint) in this channel, meaning average size in square meters, number of aisles, cooler vaults, promotional areas, gondola end displays and dealer owned coolers. Either category (like beverages) requires cooling equipment: Determine the right size and the right type of this equipment.

2 – MAP INVENTORY WITH ZONES

To place the different merchandising materials, messaging boards and displays in an ideal way, their placement should respect that each store has zones.

Use the inventory list and map it against the three principal zones that each outlet has: Transition zone, impulse zone and destination zone. (See fig. 34)

Now determine which area of the store would be most likely to be the destination for this particular category, which area of the store would be considered best for impulse purchases and quick trips, and define what should be included in the transition zone of this particular store.

Mark the floor plan with the primary occasion that should be addressed in a given location. For example, the back end of the store that is designated for fresh meat and dairy products might well be the destination area for meal related beverages.

Now that this pre-work is finalized, the different elements from the inventory can be inserted into the floor plan.

Every location, where a product is being sold, should be labeled with the primary packaging function that should be present at this area of the store. This ensures that location, consumption occasion and package function are synchronized.

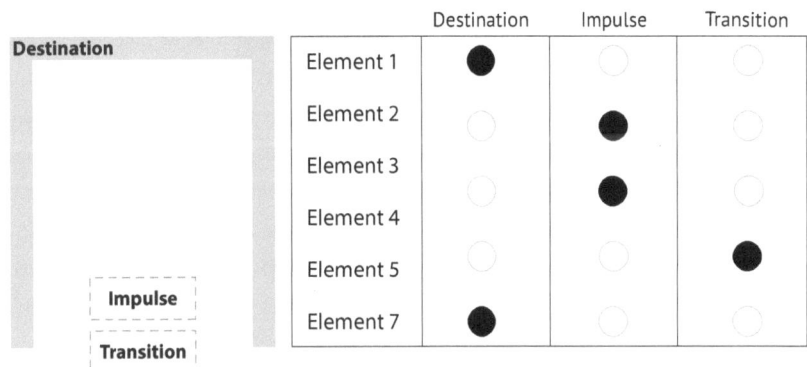

	Destination	Impulse	Transition
Element 1	●	○	○
Element 2	○	●	○
Element 3	○	●	○
Element 4	○		○
Element 5	○	○	●
Element 7	●	○	○

Fig. 34 — Inventory by zone

3 – MESSAGING

The chapter on strategy focused on permanent messaging, that is, addressing the core target group continuously by linking the primary shopping mission, the product and the consumption occasion. This strategic call to action helps to convert brand equity to purchase at the POS. Oftentimes, the permanent messaging links the brand and pack combination to a shopping mission (i.e. time to stock up on brand xxx) or to the prevailing consumption situation (i.e. visualizing a family breakfast). Permanent merchandising comes in form of outside signage, permanent displays, posters, menu boards, etc. The power of permanent merchandising comes at a cost. Permanent materials are more attractive, of higher quality and more endurable. As a result, they require higher investments and potentially setup, installment or maintenance needs.

4 - VISIBLE INVENTORY

Visible inventory (also known as disposable inventory or forward stock) is what the shopper can see on shelf. Visible inventory is different than product stored in the back-room or in warehouses.

Expanding the visible inventory in store has an immediate, positive impact on sales.

At the same time, as all shelf real estate is limited, gaining space beyond fair share (representing a brand's share of market) is one of the most challenging and also cost intensive in-store strategies. Figure 35 illustrates how the share of inventory should exceed the market share.

Unlike modern trade markets like the U.S., Japan or Europe, most developing or emerging countries do not yet operate in traditional trade with listing fees. This is partially due to a lack of knowledge and traditions, but also a result of missing sales data (mostly no scanning) or retailer insights on shelf profitability. For FMCG companies, this represents an opportunity to expand their visible inventory.

A sell in story likely to succeed ideally provides proof points to the store owner, demonstrating that increased visibility leads to a win. It is a win, because of positive store traffic impact and /or increased cross category purchases (the so called halo effect on basket size). Manufacturers should conduct field-testing in order to build such sell in stories.

A simple tool to determine directional shares of inventory is shown in figure 36: By packaging or packaging group decide whether to space them below or above their respective fair share.

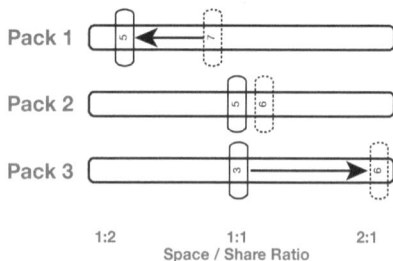

Pack 1

Pack 2

Pack 3

1:2   1:1   2:1
Space / Share Ratio

Fig. 35 — Fair pack share

This small exercise will help to allocate available shelf space across the different package functions. It also ensures that packages, which are strategically important, are spaced disproportionately.

Visible inventory has multiple drivers that all should be included in the activation floor plan:

- Number and frequency of temporary displays or end caps;
- Placement in the shelf or racks in other categories that have potential for more cross purchases;
- Permanent sales equipment, such as racks, dedicated shelves or technical equipment, such as vending machines, ice chests, coolers or dispensers.

5 – PLANOGRAMS

Simple planograms have to be created for main fixtures and large displays and other sales equipment like coolers. For large, modern customers, this is called category management and many excellent software solutions are being offered. These tools require in-depth training. Investing into people and training typically starts to pay off for five to six permanent category management projects. In developing/emerging markets with primarily unorganized trade, these tools are clearly over engineered. To achieve basic to intermediate planograms that are easy to execute, the manufacturer has to divide the given (or planned) shelf space by velocity, profitability and strategic importance (see beginning of this chapter).

A simple planogram should ensure that all "must place items" get required facings. In addition, it should set aside 20% – 40% of plano-

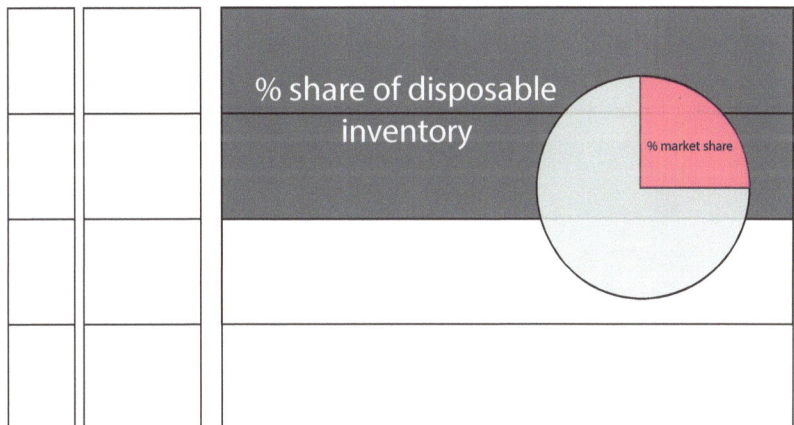

% share of disposable inventory

% market share

Fig. 36 — Share of inventory

gram space in order to allow for some flexibility for the sales person to react to specificities of each outlet (i.e. grocery store near hospital requires more room for fruit juices, etc).

6 – EQUIPMENT

Some fast moving consumer good categories, such as ice cream, beer, coffee, snacks, and even confectionery, requires cooling, heating or cooking equipment to be available. Naturally, this depends on the climate zone and the degree to which retailers provide this equipment themselves. Consumer goods that depend on sales equipment go beyond perishable goods or heated chilled food. For example, they may also include beauty products in countries with higher in-store temperatures or less reliable air conditioning.

The right amount of such sales equipment is one of the most critical investment decisions that a manufacturer has to make. Figure 37 shows a very simple, first prioritization tool. As with any investment, investments into sales equipment or messaging need to be backed up by reliable data regarding sustainable sales uplift. A simple test-control setup for field tests can help to deliver such data fast.

When calculating equipment investment level per store needs, one needs to take the following factors into consideration:

- Incremental Return on investment (ROI) per store generated by the equipment;
- Procurement, setup, depreciation and maintenance per store.

See fig. 38 for a graphical example.

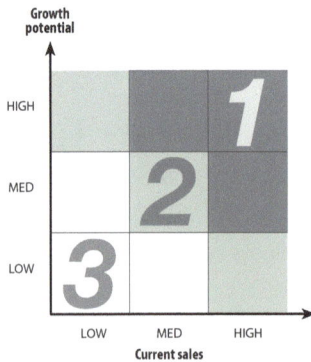

Fig. 37 — Current sales vs. potential

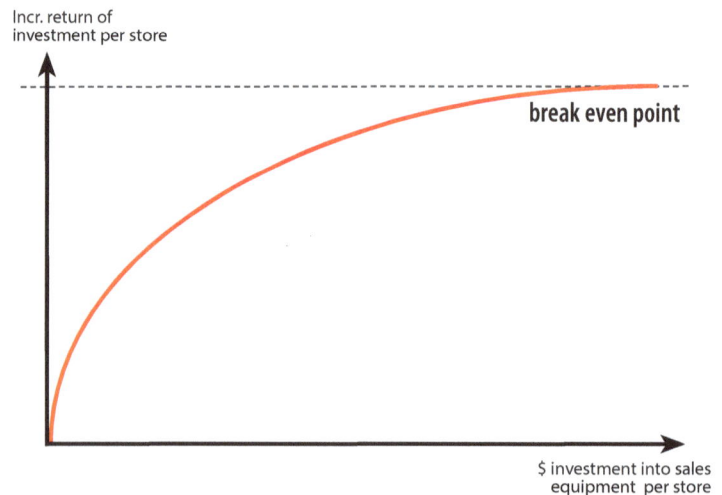

Fig. 38 — Equipment investment

7 – BUDGETING

If it has not happened yet, all investments for the different in-store items, such as displays, posters and sales equipment, need to be added up. For those items with a longer life span, the depreciation and potential maintenance and installment have to be incorporated.

The expected store budget for the next planning period should serve as a starting point. This budget is then allocated to the different channels and the sub segmentation of each channel.

When allocating in-store budgets, all channels with higher than average growth and higher than average profit should receive highest priority (see fig. 37).

One should prioritize sub segments (like Gold, Silver and Bronze) within each applicable channel. See fig. 39 for an illustrative sub segmentation.

INVEST SMARTLY

Before allocating funds to second priority channels or second priority segments, one should ensure that the budget allows to equip 100% of outlets in number one priority channels with the floor plan which had been designed for them.

Only once the top priority outlets have been fully covered start allocating budget to number two outlets.

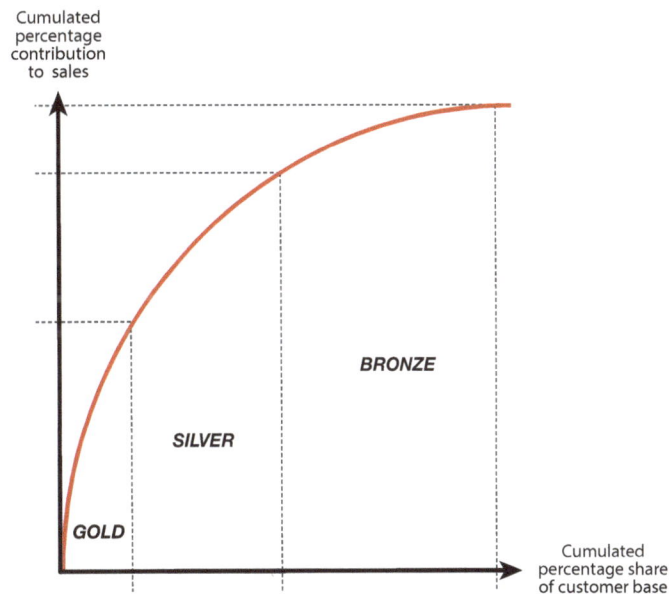

Fig. 39 — Segmentation within channel

This strict approach will lead to a situation in which some (low sales) outlets receive little or no support from the floor plan. Naturally, this is not easy to sell to the customer and, consequently, many companies start making false compromises. These companies compromise either the quality of the activation or the activation coverage of their top outlets. This results in sub-optimal returns. Therefore, planning and budgeting must be an iterative process: the planners should have a directional investment threshold in mind before they discuss in-store elements. This helps to keep the process efficient.

Once the budgeting and allocation process is finalized, it pays off to double check that chosen investments into in-store activation is still in sync with shopper profiles and growth strategy.

8 – FLOOR PLAN CREATION

Now, the map of the store can be drawn: considering the three zones discussed earlier, showing the exit/entrance locations, all aisles, gondola ends and aisle displays. Shopper flow through the store should be included, too. Locations of main fixture, displays, sales equipment and permanent messaging material must be decided on. Inside and outside view of the store is helpful to show how shoppers are addressed as they move closer to the store entrance. See fig. 40 as an example.

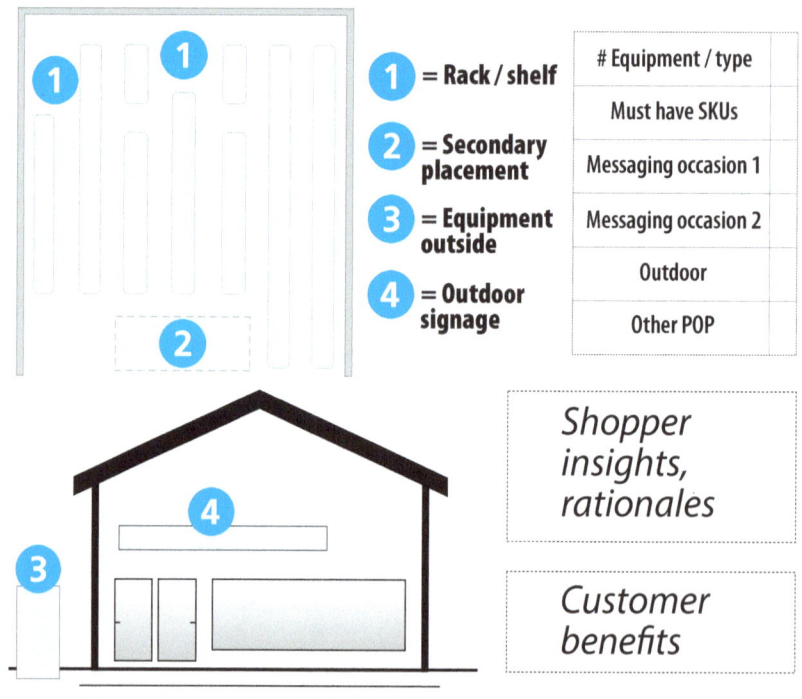

Fig. 40 — Floor plan customer proposition

9 – CUSTOMER VALUE PROPOSITION

Now that all planning has been completed, it is time to build a customer sell in story: a rationale that strongly mirrors the customer's interests versus those of the manufacturer. Objectives and strategies need to be in place to create a customer value proposition: A fact-based rationale needs to explain retailer's benefits of the designed floor plan. Wherever possible, the floor plan should be rationalized with positive impact on the product category instead of the own brand. Applying the Revenue Decomposition Tool from the customer's point of view helps to get retailer buy in, as it demonstrates how the floor plans can help to reach their own objectives. The following typical customer objectives that need to be incorporated into the value proposition are very closely related to the revenue decomposition driver:

- Consumer loyalty;
- Time spent in store;
- Average basket size;
- Trip frequency;
- Number of shopped categories.

Customers, such as Carrefour, use the same Revenue Decomposition Tool as large manufacturers in order to determine their strategy. A sell in story that demonstrates how the category (not the single brand!) grows through incidence, frequency or basket size will be welcomed.

The process of creating customer value propositions is critical for success. It not only requires shopper insights, but also sales performance of different in-store elements. This is where global consumer goods manufacturers are able to leverage their size. They can apply and cross facilitate such learning globally. A very small team of channel planning, research and front line sales people should develop customer value propositions.

10 – PILOTING

Now that the blueprint for activation has been designed, final steps towards execution must be taken.

The blueprint should be piloted to understand:

- How to convert the new floor plan into numerical execution tracking metrics;
- How to review metrics for tracking;

- How to connect customer terms and conditions to execution scores: this will help reduce merchandising costs and ensure execution quality throughout.

11 – TRAIN THE BLUE PRINT TO SALES FORCE

Sufficient capabilities to execute the blue print and the value proposition are critical for a good deployment. Applying the new blue print and the customer value proposition requires practice and many rehearsals to ensure that the aspired in-store execution can be accomplished.

The following section explains how to create and maintain execution tracking models. Therefore, at this point, it should be noted that the execution of floor plans always needs to be linked to variable sales force compensation. As a best practice, 40% of total pay should be execution based.

If changes impact the way the variable pay is being calculated, these changes have to be openly addressed and discussed in the training session mentioned above.

The sensitivity of compensation in general and the ability to track execution performance in a fair and reliable way make execution tracking (see next chapter) so important.

Now the floor plan provides the foundation for the next two important downstream assignments:

- Creating an execution tracking model (Section 8)
- Customer service model(s).

EXECUTION TRACKING MODEL

Up until now, this book has focused on commercial planning but good execution is as important as good planning. Good execution starts with building a model that tracks (in-store) execution.

An execution model needs to address these critical tasks:

- Providing unambiguous directions for executing the blue print;
- Providing clear, fair metrics for tracking;
- Setting up an execution auditing scheme;
- Providing compliance reports to sales people;
- Setting up meeting routines to review compliance and fix execution problems;
- Setting up a feedback loop for planning to continuously improve the blue print.

WHAT TO TRACK?

Tracking execution involves a substantial shift towards vertical growth, as well as a significant investment into people, IT and training. In any organization, there is a temptation to track more items than necessary or than can actually be supported. Over time and due to management changes, the number of items to be tracked has a tendency to grow. This phenomenon eventually inverses the positive sales effect of execution tracking.

Execution tracking needs to evolve in stages.

Stage 1: In the initial phase of execution tracking, sales people, auditors and supervisors should start with a lower number of tracking metrics, to which they can then add more metrics as the capability of sales support and of the sales people themselves increases. The selection of tracking metrics should be guided by the impact that each in-store element has on sales velocity.

In **Stage 1**, typically these three in-store execution metrics are tracked, as they yield the highest uplift outside of pricing activities.

1. Visible inventory (also known as "forward stock" – in case of manufacturer owned sales equipment, such as heaters or coolers, this inventory needs to be tracked separately);
2. Pricing compliance (only countries where legal);
3. Availability of a pre-defined number of "must place SKU".

In **Stage 2**, additional execution elements should be included:

1. Number of secondary placements;
2. Placement/Location of sales equipment or other secondary placements;
3. Number of facings for selected items;
4. Availability of other sales supporting material (e.g. poster and outdoor signage).

CLEAR DIRECTIONS

Clarity is achieved through simple visualized instructions and numeric directions that apply to simple tasks, i.e. provide a visual of the display, draw where to place it and list the items that belong in the display.

CLEAR METRICS

Starting with a low number of execution directions and metrics allows to become more sophisticated over time.
Criteria for good metrics should be:

- Numeric, where possible binary. For example, if target of ten facings (five points) has been missed by one, that represents zero points;
- Small time effort to measure;
- Easy to understand, measure;
- Indisputable;
- Only limited to execution, not as a management tool.

AUDITING

The execution of the floor plan through sales people requires quantitative and qualitative evaluation. Self-auditing, which is carried out by the sales person (i.e. merchandiser), who is actually in charge of the execution job, has the tendency to be overstated. Non-self auditing, which is carried out by a third party or by a separate team, is recommended.

Auditing a moving sample is more efficient than auditing all outlets.

Modern technologies, such as photo recognition, can reduce audit time significantly and will simultaneously increase audit accuracy.

Auditing should not be abused as a research tool, as the audited sample will not be sufficiently representative of the total market.

Auditing, whether conducted with internal or external resources, is a big investment. Audit frequency should be highest where the investment for in-store is highest. For example, it should be highest for group 1 customers and lowest for group 3 customers (see fig. 37).

COMPLIANCE REPORTS AND MEETING ROUTINES

Providing audit feedback and creating non-compliance lists on a daily basis is key to creating tasks for sales people. Compliance lists should be available for each store and each sales person on the morning of the next day. This helps to get the issue fixed during the next visit or even on the next day. Meeting routines are required, so that execution quality can be discussed and the line manager can set tasks.

FEEDBACK LOOP

One of the important functions of a well working execution is to feed back results and learnings to those who design the activation blue print.

Ensure meeting routines that provide feedback to those who are in charge of floor plans.

CUSTOMER SERVICE MODEL

The customer service model (CSM) describes how a company enters the market, that is, how it physically makes their products available to consumers by collaborating with retail partners.

Customer service models should include the following roles:

- Acquisition;
- Account development;
- Revenue generation;
- Delivery;
- In-store activation.

Distribution and customer service models are long-term projects. Altering the service level to customers is a critical decision. Changing job descriptions and required capabilities is a multi-year approach.

Potential alterations of a customer service model need to anticipate the following needs for the next years:

- Potential of horizontal distribution expansion (number of stores not carrying the respective brand);
- Complexity and proliferation of portfolio to sell;
- Customer demands and competitors service models;
- Ability to influence assortment, pricing and activation at the Point of Sales.

A CSM, therefore, develops over time and in accordance with the market needs described above.

A – WHOLESALE-OUTSOURCING: SIMPLE APPROACH:

The most basic CSM would be to outsource all service functions for all offerings to wholesale partners. Later in this chapter, we will discuss the role of wholesalers in complementing the own sales organization. At this point, however, we will focus on using external distribution partners instead of one's own organization.

Outsourcing customer services may promise to build up distribution faster than creating own service organizations. However, from a medium- and longer term profitability perspective, outsourcing can only be suggested if all or most of the following criteria are met:

1. A new market needs to be serviced immediately (there is insufficient time to create own structures)
2. Wholesale partners work exclusively and share customer database
3. Wholesale partners work on temporary contracts (i.e. up to three years)
4. External partners are limited to certain channels
5. External partners have access to a low number of SKU per subcategory (i.e. the strongest two-pack sizes for chocolate ice cream)
6. Manufacturers control consumer prices and retail margins

B – OWN CUSTOMER SERVICE / SALES ORGANIZATION

Following the outsourcing model, the simplest internal service organization would be to charge one sales representative with all five service roles described earlier.

As segmentation evolves, the portfolio grows and customer development becomes more important to support vertical (same-store-sales) growth, the CSM needs to evolve, too. In the final stage, technically a company would have a different CSM in the different sales channels it serves with up to one dedicated sales-expert for each of the five roles. For example: For the traditional grocery channel, a company would serve its most potential and large retailers with up to four different employees (acquisition, account development, revenue generation and in-store activation plus own delivery people).

The first step is to assess the current situation:

- Cost to serve by sales call, per capita and per unit;
- Sales calls per capita per week;
- Cost to serve per unit;
- Current skill levels and potential gaps to meet future needs;
- Which roles are currently being filled, which are not;
- Time spend in the different sales roles, including time spend driving;
- Many companies conduct "time and motion" studies every two to three years to understand the time required to deliver the different tasks to be performed.

The next step is to evaluate and simulate changes to the current model. For each simulation, calculate cost to serve and create a hypothesis on sales performance.

Work towards the final customer service model in order to serve the needs identified earlier. Then break it down into phases for gradual implementation.

Generally, the more differentiated the service roles and the more sales time, the more effective.

Companies selling very complex, technical products will tend to have higher skilled personal in Revenue Generation. Customers that are considered by consumers to be experts, have a recommending function. These customers will require higher skilled personal and long times per call. The more products are mass or generic, the lower product related skills are needed.

Any change made to the customer service model is highly sensitive and may require consultation with local labor unions. Changes of the service model often lead to changes in the number of people or changes in the level of capability requirements. Given the implications for the business, they need to be piloted and only gradually implemented. As indicated at the end of the previous chapter on "activating the blueprint," one of the critical roles of a CSM is to execute the floor plan / activation blueprint. This raises the question of compensation of sales people. Traditional models may have a fixed pay plus a variable component that depends on achieving certain metrics (i.e. monthly revenue, SKU availability, # calls/wk, etc.). More sophisticated models incorporate additional compensations for the quality of the in-store execution with up to 40% of total pay.

Pilot needs to show whether the changes in sales roles translate into changed sales performance and execution performance and, hence, compensation.

ILLUSTRATION

To achieve the annual target that TTC had set earlier and to leverage the Strategic Growth Opportunities (SGO) that were identified in the previous chapter, TTC went through a series of exercises to develop the "HOW" (that is, the strategies for cluster 1 and the other segments).

CHANNEL PROFILING

For cluster 1, they started by building a simple channel profile: income level "HIGH," urban, 70% female and household size of four. With $8.00 per trip, the average basket size is relatively small, since hypermarkets are the preferred destination for bi-weekly large basket, stock up trips. In cluster 1, higher-value, more frequent impulse purchases for kids are still soft, but also pantry filling for the next three to four days will help to grow TTC's sales. TTC created a simple table contrasting the profile for all their clusters.

4A TOOL AND SGO

Benchmarking across channels and within their international network, using the 4A tool, revealed that the key pack in cluster 1, the 1L box, requires more availability in cluster 1. In addition, this pack also needs more forward stock in store relative to fair share.

Higher value permanent signage, addressing the key consumption motivation, craving, is required to drive incidence.

In the "segmentation" session, TTC had opened the way for more targeted offerings by channel.

PACKAGING AND PRICING

Based on this fundamental change in its segmentation, TTC decided to gradually introduce channel-exclusive brands ("Daily" for cluster 2, "Excellence" in cluster 1 and modern trade, exclusive packs for food services).

"Daily" brand will move to price-differentiation in traditional grocery (10% price premium for cluster 1 vs. cluster 2). In this way, annual revenue objectives will be met and profit growth will exceed volume growth.

Using the analytic and workflow described, TTC had spent two months to develop some powerful new pack sizes that address TTC's channel and shopper insights. For cluster 2 (rural, less affluent) the "Daily" brand required a "cash outlay pack": COGS of current smallest pack, 60ml do not allow to hit the "magic consumer price point" required to work with the limited amount of cash of teen consumers, thus to attract non-users and competitive users alike.

TTC had tested an additional 45ml pack at a very competitive price point (choco flavor only) in some stores and found out that the "cannibalization," the down-trading from 60ml to 45ml, was offset by the number of new consumers that were finally able to purchase the product. The new pack at the permanent price point adds to the forward stock and helped to grow share by 1 percentage point!

CUSTOMER SERVICE MODEL / EXECUTION TRACKING MODEL

The challenging journey towards more segmentation will be supported by a new customer service model that allows for control and direct influence of the most important retailers.

In the previous year, TTC piloted multiple customer service models and utilized those results to come up with an improved Customer Service model, where TOP 80% of traditional grocery outlets will be served directly (instead of some wholesale service).

Furthermore, TTC will start to move away from a route-based approach, where one sales representative covered all five service roles. Instead, TTC will start to separate its sales force by channel. Incremental costs of two sales representatives working in the same area have tested to be overcompensated when sales people spent more time with their strongest retailers. Every four weeks the top 20% of cluster 1 outlets will start to receive consultation from a specialized account developer. In addition, the current sales representative that also takes care of the right merchandising will make weekly visits. Delivery takes place two times per week.

In addition to changed roles in the customer service model, TTC decided to hire five "auditors" that cover 30% of all serviced cluster 1 outlets with at least four visits per year.

ACTIVATION BLUEPRINT

For each cluster and channel, an activation blueprint was created and budgeted based on the pilots that had been carried out. The pilots showed an average revenue uplift of 25% when the "activation blueprint" was at a level of 80%.

Customers will be offered an incremental 1% year-end discount, if the average compliance rate with the "activation blueprint" was 80% or higher. At the same time, sales representatives are offered a bonus of up to 10% if all their audited outlets achieve an average execution score of at least 80.

The "activation blueprint" for cluster 1 included four deliverables that are being audited:

1. Five "must place items" available at all times with at least two facings;
2. One TTC branded ice cream cooler in good position;
3. One permanent signage / board;
4. Forward stock: +5 percentage points above current TTC share in channel.

TACTICS

»Strategy without tactics is the slowest route to victory. Tactics without strategy is the noise before defeat.«

— Sun Tzu, The Art of War

WHERE THE RUBBER HITS THE ROAD

This chapter is structured into the following groups of tactical measures:

- (Consumer-) Promotion, (tactical) pricing;
- (Tactical) Packaging;
- (Promotion) Merchandising;
- (Temporary) Messaging;
- (Vertical) Availability;
- SKU Rationalization.

Tactics is where the rubber hits the road. Oftentimes, commercial associates in developing or emerging markets focus too early on tactics when building out their commercial business plan. Large global consumer goods manufacturers, however, have demonstrated that tactics really should be placed at the end of the commercial planning process. Conducting the required diligence of segmentation and strategy will not only make the tactical measures more powerful, but it will also help to reduce the resources spent on developing tactical initiatives.

Chapter Three outlined how to develop a strategy by combining vertical and horizontal strategies (**A**ffordability, **A**vailability, **A**ccuracy and **A**ctivation – the **4As**) with strategic growth opportunities (SGO), using Revenue drivers: Incidence, Transaction and Amount (see fig. 26).

Strategies now need to be mapped with potential tactics. Figure 41 maps 4A, SGO and revenue drivers with tactical measures. Also, drivers coming out of the Revenue Decomposition Tool (see previous chapter) should be mapped with potential tactics.

(CONSUMER) PROMOTION – (TACTICAL) PRICING

Consumer sales promotion will remain the hottest and most frequently used tactical measure in FCMG companies. Competitive actions and internal short-term volume pressure make sales promotion the hottest topic in between annual planning cycles. Four questions are debated: the frequency of promotions (e.g. 26 times/yr), the depth of the consumer price discount, invoicing to customers and the promotion mechanic itself.

The percentage that promotional volume contributes to total volume is an indicator for the degree of saturation and competitiveness in a market – in combination with a high share of (organized) modern retail formats. Highly competitive markets and mature, saturated categories will have the deepest and most frequent price promotions.

Calculating the Return Of Investment (ROI) of promotions is a science in itself, as the number of moving parts is high:

- Consumer price elasticity can shift depending on seasonality or geography;
- Competitive actions cannot be projected;
- Retailers attempting to recruit shoppers by selling items at aggressive, low prices (also known as loss leader concept).

The general approach to financially sound promotions or self-liquidating promotions is to increase promotional spending (lost margins per unit), as long as the incremental profit (incremental volume mul-

Opportunity		SGO from Revenue Decomposition (What)			
		Incidence	Transaction	Amount (Vol)	Amount ($)
4A tool (How)	(vertical) availability	have recruitment packs fully available, where non users shop	have "daily" pack sizes for frequent purchase available	make value packs fully available, where stock up shopping prevails	have "upscale"/ high revenue packs available
	activation	messaging, displays targeting new users	Displays, sales equipment, adjacencies, where other daily items are purchased	secondary placements and messaging using price offs, bundle packs, overfills, multi-buys. Forward stock on retailer side	displays, sales equipment adressing impulse purchase
	affordability	pricing allowing new users to afford recruitment packs	pricing that fits daily purchase amount plus permanent mssg of EDLP (every day low price)	overfills, price messaging	
	accuracy	Segment into lower Socio economic zones to allow for consumer prices matching lower purchase power		develop tailor made value packs	Segment into high income areas to allow for consumer prices and packages addressing higher purchase power

Fig. 41 — Tactics by revenue driver

tiplied by margin per unit) is able to offset it. See fig. 43 for a graphic example.

Profit of promoted volume

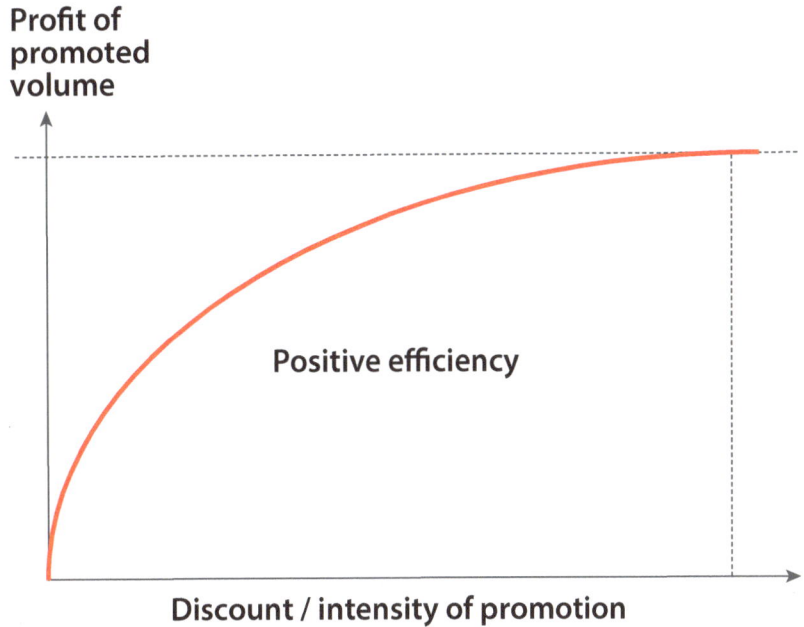

Fig. 43 — Promo efficiency

At times, however, manufacturers openly accept promotions with negative ROI. This is done with the intent of either buying volume to achieve certain targets or buying market share. Market share is often seen as an investment into future profits. Share growth is expected to translate, with a delay, into an opportunity to charge higher consumer prices and, hence, generate profits.

Tip: With an increasing contribution of modern trade in emerging markets, spending on consumer (price) promotions for FMCG will increase in these markets.

Promotional efficiency is a topic all of its own and well covered in marketing literature, which is why this book will only provide some high-level tools. FMCG companies should be very careful not to over-use the price promotion tool at an early stage. As long as saturation has not been reached, FMCG companies should opt for other commercial tools in order to achieve organic growth

The potential number of options for each promotion type and the ways to communicate the promotion are almost unlimited. In fact, each product category has a slightly different set of promotions. New communication technologies and devices continuously add new opportunities. For this reason, this book does not evaluate (consumer) promotions in more depth.

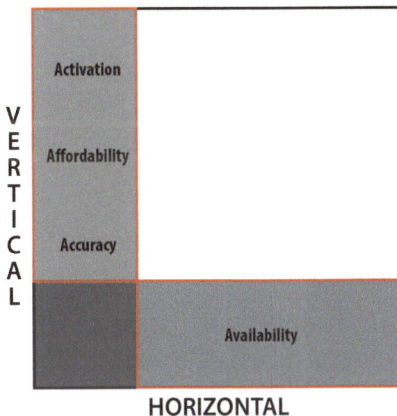

Fig. 42 — Horizontal / vertical

A simple grouping of most relevant (consumer) promotion mechanics for packaged consumer goods include:

- Single item (consumer) price promotion;
- Multi-buy (i.e. buy five, pay four);
- (Temporary) Multipacks at discounted price;
- Packs with dual use or with high attractiveness (i.e. champagne packaging serving also as an attractive cooler);
- BOGOF (Buy one, get one free);
- Add-on promotions (i.e. item plus a gift);
- Overfill/oversize (regular size increased by certain percentage at same price);
- Sweepstakes – winners are chosen by luck for a range of prices;
- Contests – i.e. consumers send in answers, drawings or similar;
- Mass coupons (either printed or on-line);
- Personalized loyalty schemes – i.e. club card holders receive targeted offers based on their shopping history.

Consumer promotion becomes more effective if supported with mass media (also known as "above the line"), and/or "below the line". Examples for "below the line" would be:

- Weekly leaflets;
- In-store messaging;
- In-store TV;
- Email or text messaging;
- Free standing displays;
- Sampling;
- Promotion ladies;
- End cap displays;
- Shelf frames.

RETAIL PROMOTION

To support consumer promotion, FMCG companies often use retail promotions, that is, activities targeting its retail customers and their staff:

- Time bound discounts;
- Customer staff incentives (gifts, trips for a certain behavior or tasks);
- Rebates linked to certain purchase quantities;
- Discounts or cash incentives related to displaying items in store in the desired way or in a preferred location;
- Incentives for recommending selected items/brands (i.e. mystery man promotions).

Incentives offered to the own sales people often support consumer and retail promotions.

TACTICAL PACKAGING

Packaging is primarily a strategic decision (see Chapter Three). However, depending on the complexity of change or the level of manufacturing implications, packaging can become tactical when used for promotions. Illustrative promotional packaging mechanics include:

- Temporary (in/out) overfill packaging (e.g. 60 grams instead of 50gram chocolate bar);
- Temporary pack design supporting a mass media campaign or featuring large events or celebrities;
- Collections – pack design series to trigger collecting a series, i.e. series of packs, labels, featuring a soccer player prior to FIFA soccer world cup;
- For secondary packaging – specially designed boxes, trays or containers. Hybrid usage of secondary packaging, i.e. metal boxes as storage

TIP

Leveraging the vast amount of shopper data that becomes available through scan and loyalty card data , as well as online profiles, helps to target most valuable shoppers with more precision and to spend promotion budgets more efficiently.

Digital promotion mechanics will become the discipline of the future in emerging markets. While smart phone penetration and bandwidth increases at a fast pace, traditional promotion execution in a growing number of very small convenience retail outlets becomes increasingly challenging.

Examples for digital promotion mechanics could be: Text messages, NFC messages or upsizing email QR coupons for special seasonal occasions, crosspurchase coupons sent to smartphones before orduring shopping trips, and so on ...

Promotion investment often is the single largest item in commercial or marketing budgets. This requires promotions to be prioritized by their return on investment and discipline in linking them back to channel objectives.

The investment will differ across industries and retail environments. An easy way to shortlist potential tactics is by grouping them into (a) return on investment and (b) ease/speed of execution. See fig. 44

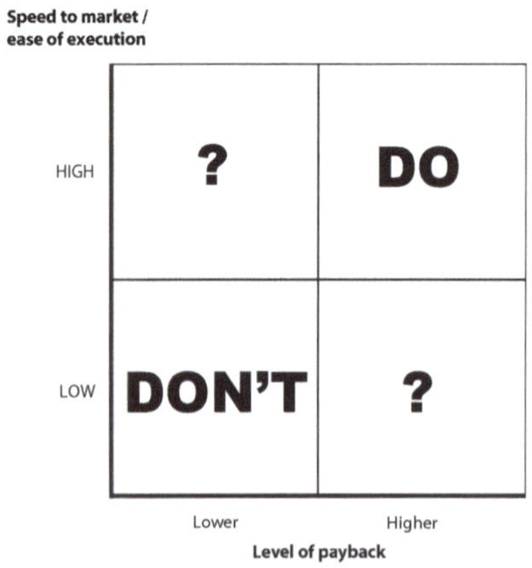

Speed to market / ease of execution

HIGH	**?**	**DO**
LOW	**DON'T**	**?**
	Lower	Higher

Level of payback

Fig. 44 — Investment x execution matrix

MESSAGING

Messaging describes the practice of communicating to shoppers through means of in-store communication. Messaging can be grouped into temporary and permanent messaging. Messaging can be sent off-line (printed media) or on-line (messages or mails) to mobile phones.

TEMPORARY

Temporary messaging typically supports in-store promotions and national mass media supported campaigns at the Point of Sales (POS). This often includes off-line / printed media: posters, displays or display headers, stickers, banners and so forth.

PERMANENT

Permanent messaging (covered in Chapter Three on strategy) links the product to a shopping mission (e.g. time to stock up on ice cream) or to the prevailing consumption situation. Permanent merchandising comes in the form of outside signage, permanent displays or posters, menu boards, etc. It typically involves high costs and complex setup.

VERTICAL AVAILABILITY

Extending vertical distribution may be considered the least cost intensive tactic. In contrast, horizontal expansion typically asks for more resources on the ground, external support or the dropping of other priorities.

In the chapters on activation blueprint, the concept of "must place items" was introduced. Vertical availability needs to focus on full availability of these "must place items," as those items have been carefully selected as the "orchestra" of brands, pack sizes and price points to maximize revenues. Only if the full "orchestra" is available the "concert" can begin. With organized accounts (e.g. supermarket or convenience store chains) "must place items," as well as new launches, are typically part of the annual business planning documents. Both manufacturer, as well as customer headquarters, have a mutual interest in placing all contracted / "must place items" in all of the outlets.

Figure 45 illustrates how to summarize the opportunities for (vertical) growth according to each of the Must place/ contracted SKU. The revenue potential of closing distribution gaps can be calculated as follows by SKU: Annual rate of sale (average revenue generated per 1% numeric distribution [not per outlet!!], where item is on shelf) multiplied with percentage gap of current numeric distribution versus 100%.

With organized accounts, as in supermarkets, the vertical availability needs to match with the contractual agreements. In traditional grocery, which prevails in emerging markets, all items that have been classified as mandatory need to have full vertical availability in the respective channel. See fig. 42.

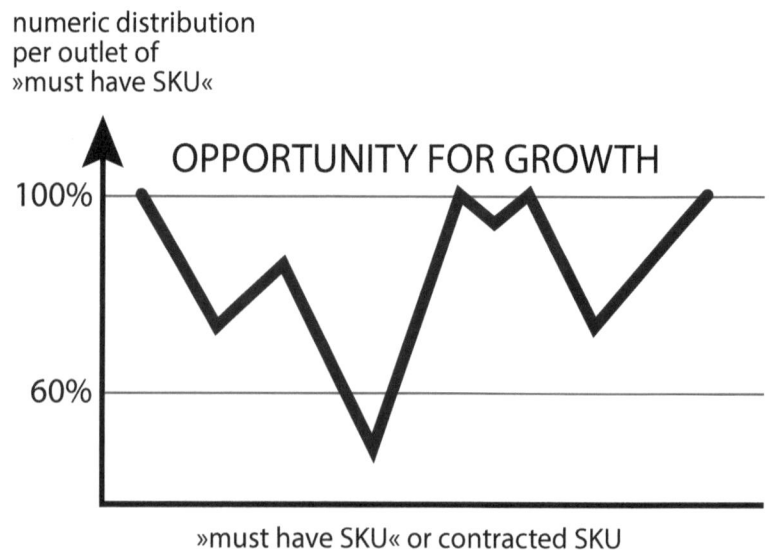

numeric distribution
per outlet of
»must have SKU«

OPPORTUNITY FOR GROWTH

100%

60%

»must have SKU« or contracted SKU

Fig. 45 — Opportunity for growth

ILLUSTRATION

Emergia has 1,000 7-Eleven convenience stores that contractually list TTC's 1-liter chocolate ice cream.

Nielsen market research tells TTC that this item has 80% numeric availability in 7-Eleven and 90% weighted distribution.

TTC has used 7-Eleven POS data to find out that the annual rate of sales of the respective SKU is $20,000 per store where currently on shelf and estimated about $1,500 per "missing" outlets.

1% of distribution equals ten outlets, hence the missed revenue opportunity is 10 x $1,500 = $15,000 for 1 percentage point gap. If the total distribution gap of 20% would be closed, the total growth opportunity would be 20 x $15,000 = $300,000 per annum.

SKU RATIONALIZATION

SKU rationalization could be considered either a strategy or a tactic. As it should be an annual exercise, this book will treat it as a tactical measure.

As SKU proliferation creates complexity and hidden costs, each SKU has to be reviewed every year. New items receive a period of six to nine months of monitoring before they are included into the SKU rationalization.

Many large CPG companies have a tail of up to 80% of their SKU that cumulatively contribute less than 10%. At the same time, sometimes only three to five SKUs have a cumulative sales contribution of 30% or more.

The following are principle drivers of the number of SKUs:

- Number of categories covered (i.e. portfolio expansion), which is not discussed in this book;
- Degree of segmentation;
- Insufficient assortment management;
- New launches that are being added to existing assortment without discontinuing items;
- Strong retail accounts asking for exclusive items. This is more relevant in markets with a dominating role of modern trade accounts, such as Australia.

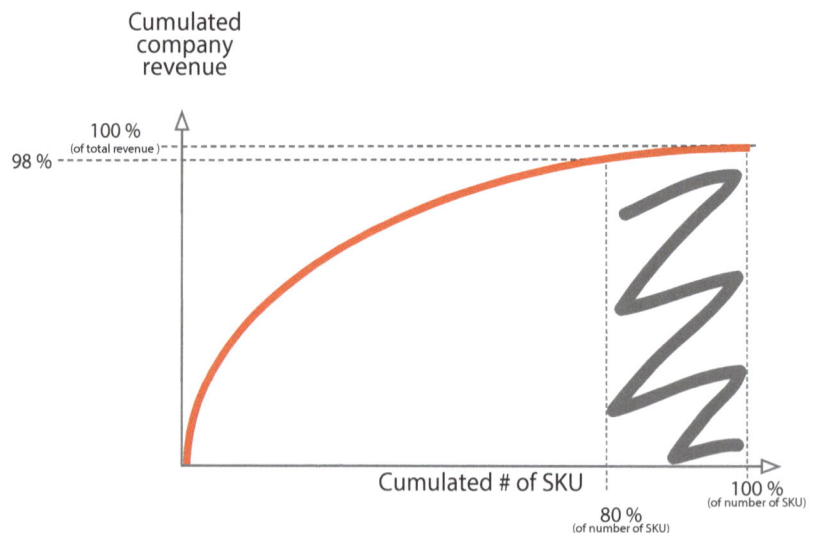

Fig. 46 — SKU rationalization

Improving assortment management capabilities and routines are among the key priorities. A rule among large companies with high SKU complexity is the following: For each new SKU, one SKU has to be discontinued. In this way, the status quo is maintained.

The second learning is to discontinue the bottom 2% of SKUs each year. In most cases, these bottom 2% (in a cumulated sales ranking) contribute less than 1% of total sales.

The third and maybe most effective way to manage the number of SKUs is to rigorously implement the concept of "must place items" (see the chapter on packaging and pricing) by channel. This practice provides a short list of optional items that sales people can list in their stores in addition to the "must place items."

ILLUSTRATION

PRICING

With strategies in place, TTC now develops a series of tactical measures that collectively bring those strategies to life.

For all modern trade accounts, the number of annual consumer price offs for the 1l pack were agreed upfront. It has been agreed upon that discounts would not exceed 30% - unless jointly decided. Price promotions always go together with large secondary coolers and messaging outside the main aisle for two weeks, supported by advertisement in the retailers weekly leaflet.

TACTICAL PACKAGING

As part of the joint business plan with chained retailers, TTC offered temporary and exclusive packaging to some of their accounts. To boost sales during summer and Christmas season, the three modern trade retailers each received distinct overfill packs to be sold at 5% below price per ml of the 1l pack.

These seasonal packs were again supported with seasonal messaging in store.

AVAILABILITY

The list of "must place items" and their facings were shared and agreed upon with TTC's key accounts. TTC offers accounts an additional 1% year-end rebate if they ensure that the "must place items" are permanently on shelf and that agreed promotions are fully executed.

SKU RATIONALIZATION

During the first four years of its operations in Emergia, TTC launched about twenty new SKUs each year, including new flavors, new pack sizes and some new promotional items.

During their business planning, they confirmed what everybody had already assumed: only a few SKUs were "strong performers," while nobody has dared to touch a long tail of "under-performers."

The new segmentation and the new split of packs and prices created a great opportunity to clean up TTC's portfolio. Using the provided tools, TTC identified that out of their 100 SKUs, 10 SKUs represented about 40% of sales and the weakest 30 SKUs combined stood only for 1.5% of sales. For each SKU, a switching recommendation was developed. Then, scrap cost were estimated. Finally, thirty items were discontinued over a course of three months.

EXECUTION

The changes in TTC's execution tracking model had been explained in the strategy illustration.

To determine the outlets to be audited in the agreed frequency, a (secret) list of outlets was generated. Each sales representative received a full day of training on the "activation blueprint," how to order the materials required and how the auditors track the execution. It was explained to them how the final execution score (a composite score) will be calculated and how this score then translates into the sales person's year-end bonus.

»Plans are only good
intentions unless they
immediately degenerate
into hard work.«

— Peter Drucker

SCORECARD

Now we have reached the final step of the Closed Commercial Loop™. As Peter Drucker said: »What's measured improves.«

In spite of daily challenges, competitive actions and customer requests, metrics are essential in modern commercial work. Staying on track is required.

This chapter is divided into the following sections:

- How to set SMART objectives.
- (Right) number of metrics;
- Simple scorecard format;

In this book, "KBI" and "metrics" refer to two different things. Chapter Two on objectives displayed a potential list of low-level and high-level KBI (see fig. 12 and fig. 13). This book will not add to these at this point.

SMART OBJECTIVES

Following our approach, all metrics will be **SMART** by default:

- **S**pecific;
- **M**anageable;
- **A**ctionable;
- **R**elevant;
- **T**ime based.

It is suggested to set up a quarterly (or at least biannually) review of this scorecard. Start three months before the commercial plan for the following year is due and add a checkpoint halfway through the business period.

In order to close the commercial loop and connect to the initial objectives, a consolidation of metrics is required.

To enable consolidation, it is important not to use different metrics for the different strategies and tactics.

The connectors, sitting between tactics and metrics, are designed to graphically confirm this and ensure that no tactic is without a success metric.

NOTE

Build your metrics in such a way that they link back to your objectives (Chapter Two) by using the connectors – see fig. 27.

This figure demonstrates how to consolidate a high number of measures. The commercial loop can be closed only if all measures can be linked back to the initial strategic objectives.

NUMBER OF METRICS

A good way to imagine the steps from channel objectives to setting metrics is an organization chart with an increasing number of branches going down.

In the chapter on objectives, high-level KBI (i.e. national share, ROIC) were allocated top-down during strategic planning and low-level KBI were created in an interactive top-down – bottom-up process during operational planning.

Typically, a company would have two or three channel level strategies, which in turn are supported by a number of tactics. Therefore, the total number of metrics is a multiplication of (channel) strategies and respective tactics.

This chapter solely focuses on operational planning, hence overlaying low-level KBI values with performance metrics for each of the tactics developed in the previous section.

NOTE

Use connectors to build your tactics metrics in such a way that they link back to low-level and high-level KBI – see fig. 47 and fig. 27.

Figure 47 shows the principle way of mapping various tactics measures (i.e. number of incremental sales equipment leading to incremental revenue) with low-level metrics (i.e. total planned revenue growth).

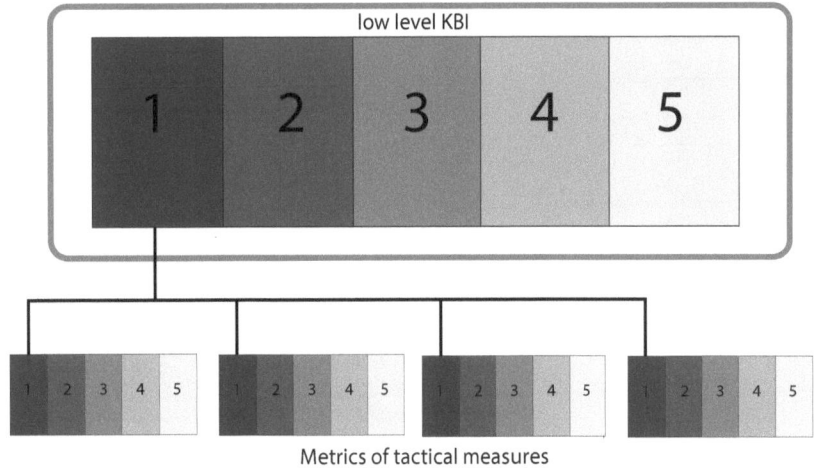

Fig. 47 — Metrics mapping

SIMPLE SCORECARD FORMAT

The choice of metrics is determined by the tactical measure. A few illustrative metrics that are often used would be

- Coupon/ QR code redemption code;
- Repurchase rate;
- Basket size;
- Purchase incidence.

A scorecard should be created on a channel/account level. A simple table – vertically the various tactics and their corresponding metric, horizontally actual and planned performance.

ILLUSTRATION

The following short example, based on our fictitious ice cream company TTC, will make this mapping process less abstract:

In the illustration to the "objectives" chapter, TTC's annual growth target for cluster/channel three was set at +6% (among other objectives). In the same example, this channel target was then allocated to TTC's "soft ice" category, which allowed for a +7% growth rate or an additional 7 million dollars added to last year's revenue of 100 million dollars.

When next year's tactics for soft ice in cluster 1 were agreed upon, three primary tactics were developed:

1. One incremental soft ice machine in 1,000 stores, each generating $2,000 per annum and collectively totaling two million dollars,
2. Closing the availability gap of soft ice cream in 10% of outlets, each percentage point equaling $100,000 per annum, totaling in one million dollars.

Assuming that per capita soft ice cream consumption – Applying last years weather conditions, income growth and consumption days, it can be assumed that per capita soft ice cream consumption will "naturally" grow by 4%, or four million dollars. In this case, the above-mentioned tactics need to generate the missing three million dollars, which they do.

The metrics to be applied to the two tactics could be:

1. Incremental machine implementations,
2. Availability improvement soft ice in cluster 1 of +10%.

THE HOSHIN TOOL

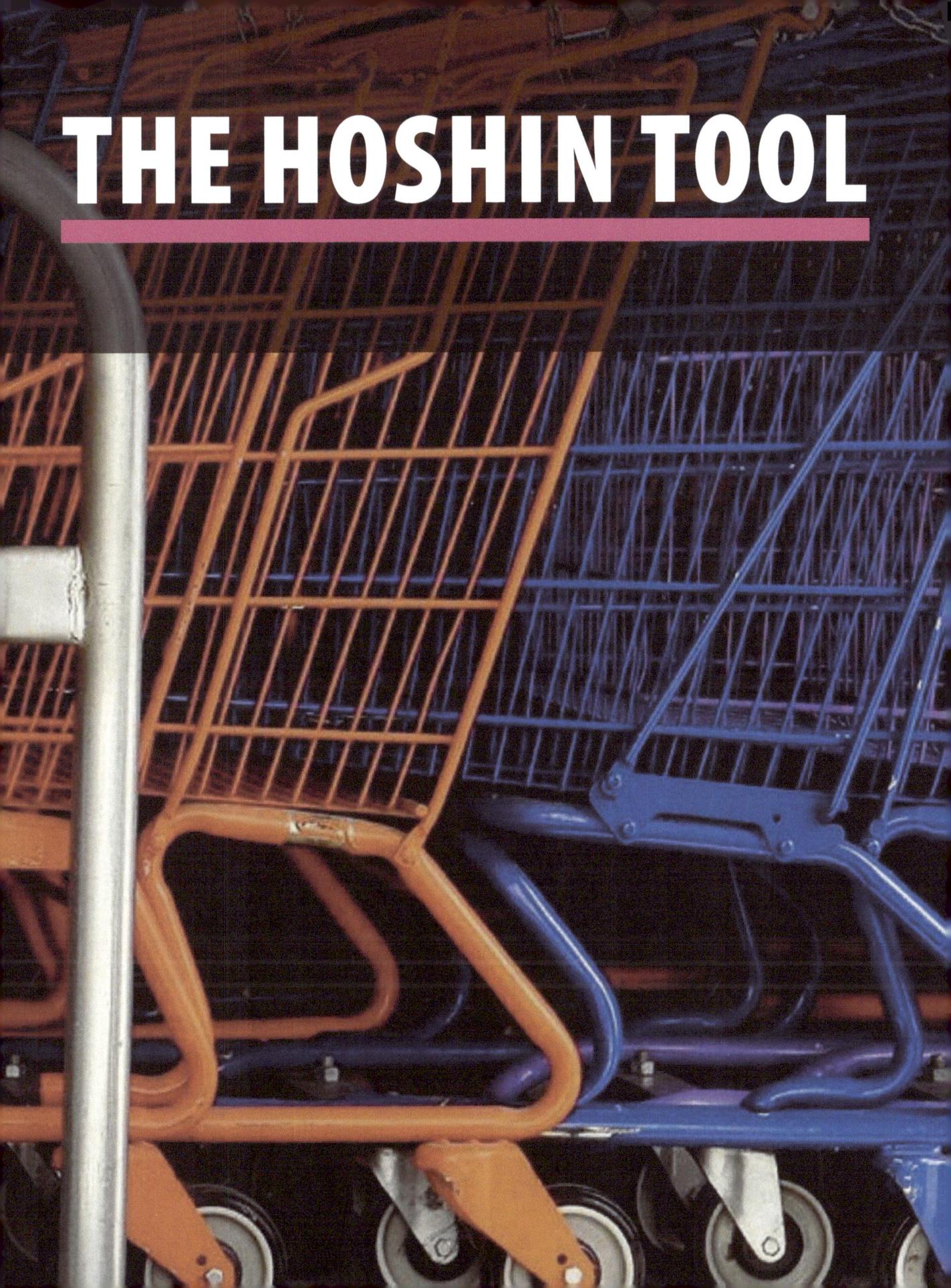

»In the modern world of
business, it is useless
to be a creative, original
thinker unless you
can also sell what you
create.«

— David Ogilvy

A PRACTICAL TOOL

We have now discussed all steps of an operational, commercial plan for one or multiple channels. Starting with the review of segmentation (1) to metrics monitoring the performance of individual tactics or execution of in-store activation (5).

A small spreadsheet tool will connect all previous work streams (see fig. 48) and conclude this book.

The spreadsheet tool will help to summarize the commercial plan on one page, allowing a line of sight all the way from high-level objectives to the performance of individual promotions. The spreadsheet, inspired by Hoshin-Kanri, will support this work. The Japanese word Hoshin means "pointing the direction," while Kanri translates to management or control. It is needless to say that each of the numbers and statements in the spreadsheet will be backed up with more detail, illustrations and research. However, having all activities on one page allows

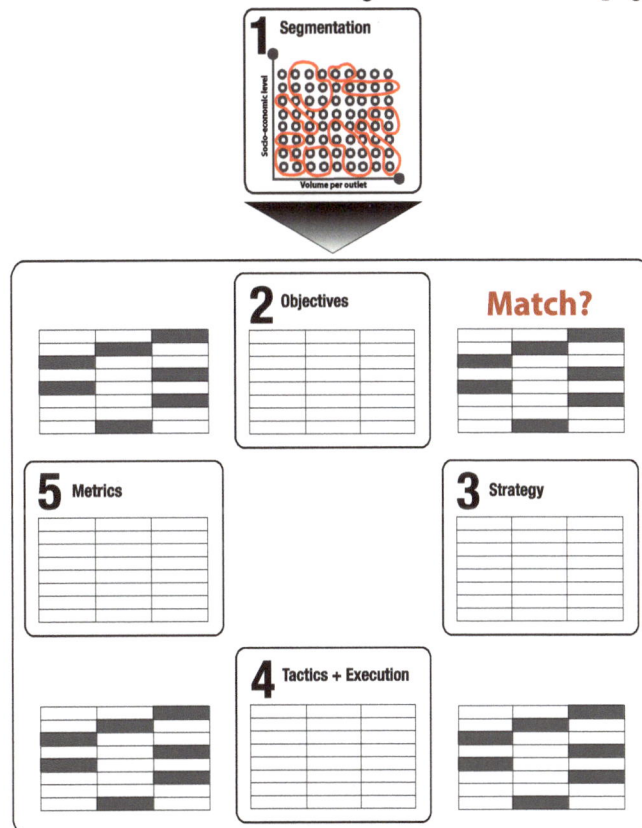

Fig. 48 — Hoshin matrix

oversight in an increasingly complex commercial world. Download a generic Hoshin spreadsheet with QR 24.

As all businesses are becoming increasingly dynamic, small to medium planning adjustments have to be conducted throughout the year. In fact, any good commercial planner should, at least, review channel objectives, strategies and tactics on a quarterly basis.

Even though the annual plan may have been very well designed, learnings and results will often require adjustments to the annual plan. The spreadsheet tool facilitates this adaptation process with a fact-based and metric approach.

Hoshin-Kanri is a simple, yet sophisticated planning approach used by many global corporations like Bank of America, Dell, HP, Nissan, Sega, Toyota and many others.

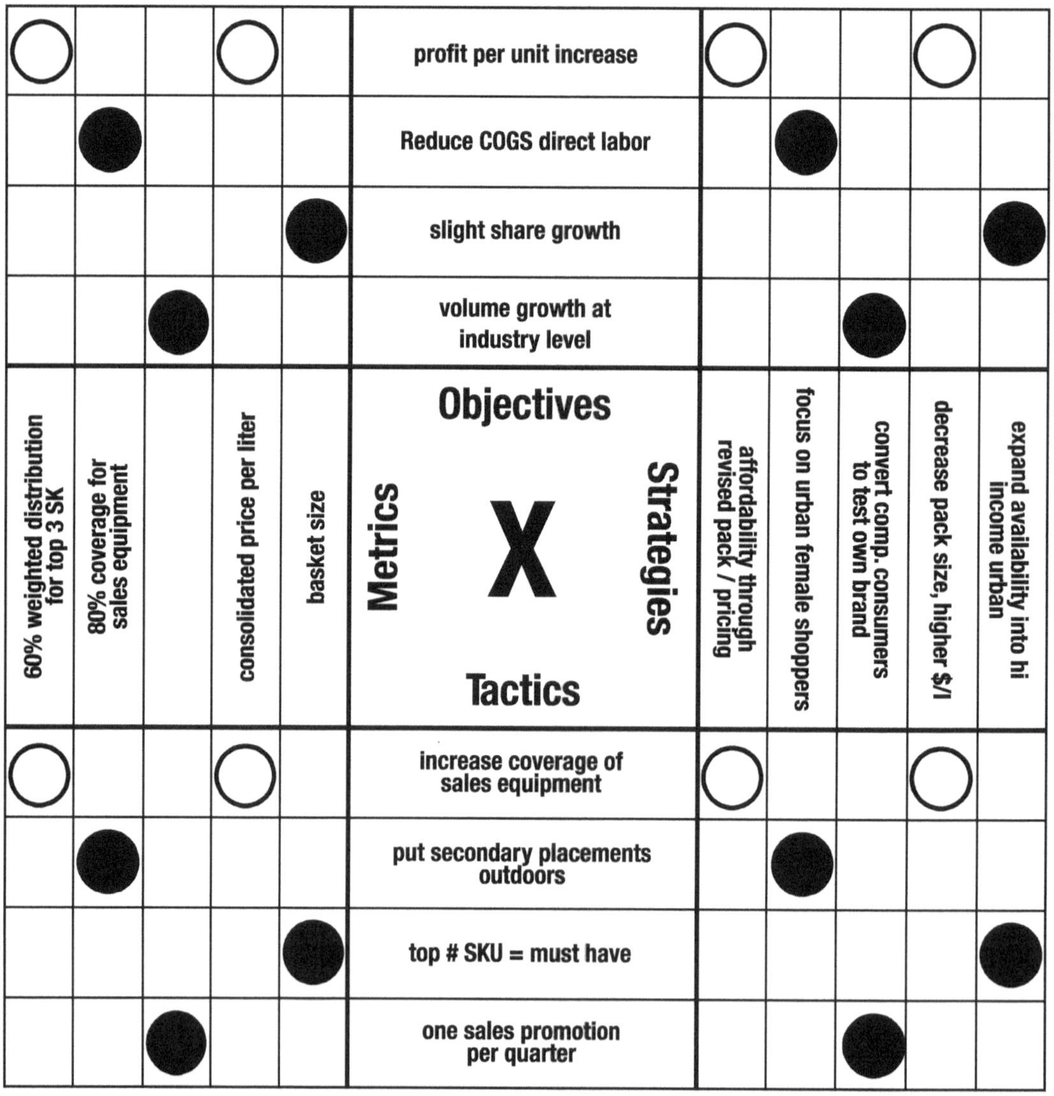

The matrix (X-matrix) is organized around a central **X** with **Objectives** (top), **Tactics** (bottom), **Metrics** (left) and **Strategies** (right).

Metrics (left columns):
- 60% weighted distribution for top 3 SK
- 80% coverage for sales equipment
- consolidated price per liter
- basket size

Strategies (right columns):
- affordability through revised pack / pricing
- focus on urban female shoppers
- convert comp. consumers to test own brand
- decrease pack size, higher $/l
- expand availability into hi income urban

Objectives (top rows) — correlations:

Objective	60% weighted dist. top 3 SK	80% coverage sales equip.	consolidated price/liter	basket size	affordability revised pack/pricing	focus urban female shoppers	convert comp. consumers	decrease pack size, higher $/l	expand availability hi income urban
profit per unit increase	○		○			○		○	
Reduce COGS direct labor		●				●			
slight share growth				●					●
volume growth at industry level			●				●		

Tactics (bottom rows) — correlations:

Tactic	60% weighted dist. top 3 SK	80% coverage sales equip.	consolidated price/liter	basket size	affordability revised pack/pricing	focus urban female shoppers	convert comp. consumers	decrease pack size, higher $/l	expand availability hi income urban
increase coverage of sales equipment	○		○			○		○	
put secondary placements outdoors		●				●			
top # SKU = must have				●					●
one sales promotion per quarter		●					●		

Fig. 49 — Hoshin spreadsheet

SET-UP OF SPREADSHEET

QR 24 Excel

Create a large spreadsheet document (for the principle structure see fig. 49) – or utilize a generic Hoshin spreadsheet (QR 24).

Create a box consisting of two columns and four lines for each of the book's four central chapters:

1. Objectives;
2. Strategies;
3. Tactics and Execution;
4. Metrics.

Each box is constructed out of two columns:

- First column describes the What,
- Second column the optional metric. Example: National volume share brand x; xx %.

Arrange these boxes similar to figure 49, so that the boxes touch each other on one corner, forming a "circle."

Add more boxes (same format: two columns and x lines) to fill the upper left and upper right corners, as well as the lower left and lower right corners. This will convert the circle format into a square format.

This tool connects all annual commercial planning and execution work, ranging from objectives to tactical metrics and execution tracking. It is designed to support commercial leaders in business reviews and prior to the next planning cycle.

OUTLOOK

»Sometimes when you innovate, you make mistakes. It is best to admit them quickly, and get on with improving your other innovations.«

— Steve Jobs

CONCLUDING COMMENTS

A CASE FOR CHANGE compiles and merges the authors' personal experiences with proven business and academic teachings. The book stays mostly at a conceptual level to cover a maximum of FMCG categories. However, at the same time, it provides many concrete examples that mirror today's reality, as well as a suite of tools and checklists that (with some adjustment) are applicable to the majority of companies' strategic and operational planning.

Commercial work used to be very close to sales and, as a result, it has been considered a social science. However, selling FMCG no longer only depends on having the best sales people building the best relationships — the art and science of the point of purchase has become more important over time . This evolution will continue to change the way in which commercial work is planned and executed.

Today, even developing markets start to have reduced rates of (horizontal) outlet expansion. Consequently, growth sources need to come from more revenue from the same number of shoppers in the same number of outlets.

Basic needs are being covered fast, meaning that an increasing number of developing markets will soon reach saturation of some consumer goods categories.

In order to continue to grow, Revenue Management and commercial segmentation, meaning higher revenues with the same number of transactions, same number of shoppers and same number of customers, becomes critical.

Following the principles of Revenue Management, this book is designed to build a foundation for healthy and sustainable growth.

Today, the world's most successful FMCG companies succeed with a mix of creating awareness and demand for their brands, being great partners and converting brand power into purchases at the Point of Sales.

Executing plans that are becoming increasingly sophisticated is key. The good news is that technology will help to keep investments moderate. Wide availability of broadband coverage and smart phones will allow for improved account development, as well as continuous tracking of the tailored execution at the POS, through greatly improved scanning and recognition technology.

As businesses become larger and more complex and as portfolios increase, the suggested Hoshin spreadsheet provides a line of sight that ensures that companies' high-level objectives will be met with a high degree of efficiency.

All the best for you and your business!

The author warmly welcomes any feedback or experience.

QR 25 Ingo Bernhardt

At the end of this book we would like to call your attention to our website **www.case-4-change.com** which may offer not only more information and material concerning all we have discussed in this textbook but also explains how to access our webinars and tutorials.

ABOUT THE AUTHOR

Ingo Bernhardt is Director of Customer and Commercial Leadership at The Coca-Cola Company in South Korea. Since 1989, he has held various leading commercial, sales and marketing roles with Coca-Cola, Nestlé and Mars. Over the last twenty-five years he has worked and lived in four different continents. Up to today he has been in charge of commercial projects in thirty-eight countries, each with a financial impact of multiple million US dollars. He also has lectured at various business schools.

APPENDIX

»There is no time for
cut-and-dried monotony.
There is time for work.
And time for love. That
leaves no other time!«

— Coco Chanel

SOURCES INTERNET

goo.gl/IJIzcN
http://www.bain.com/publications/articles/are-you-ahead-of-the-curve-in-emerging-markets.aspx

goo.gl/JxcauN
http://www.mckinsey.com/insights/urbanization/urban_world

goo.gl/QClDOu
http://www.bain.com/publications/articles/getting-ready-to-profit-from-the-next-billion-consumers.aspx

goo.gl/Q5Ydoj
http://csi.mckinsey.com/knowledge_by_region/global/finding_profits_and_growth_in_emerging_markets

goo.gl/fkYR5H
http://www.bain.com/publications/articles/eight-great-trillion-dollar-growth-trends-to-2020.aspx

goo.gl/c8GZoG
http://www.bbc.co.uk/news/business-18503627

goo.gl/vFhsoA
http://www.voxeu.org/article/new-measure-global-middle-class

goo.gl/fR5ONn
http://www.bain.com/publications/articles/eight-great-trillion-dollar-growth-trends-to-2020.aspx

goo.gl/XK9x3O
http://csi.mckinsey.com/knowledge_by_region/global/finding_profits_and_growth_in_emerging_markets

goo.gl/gnzhWO
http://hbr.org/2011/10/the-ceo-of-heinz-on-powering-growth-in-emerging-markets/ar/1

goo.gl/C2XVpM
http://www.forbes.com/2010/01/29/muhtar-kent-co-ca-cola-leadership-citizenship-sustainability.html

goo.gl/ksi6Ca
http://www.ens-newswire.com/ens/jun2007/2007-06-05-07.asp

goo.gl/6jertO
http://www.greenretaildecisions.com/news/2012/11/08/coca-cola-reaches-for-water-neu

goo.gl/QreyiT
http://au.ibtimes.com/articles/512143/20131008/coca-cola-coke-ekocenters-water-power-business.htm#.UnSI35H99Y4

www.ingramcontent.com/pod-product-compliance
Lightning Source LLC
Chambersburg PA
CBHW041454210326
41599CB00005B/242